Abundance of Grace

Lynn Kavanagh

Copyright

Dedication

This book is dedicated to my children. I can honestly say that there has never been a day since you both were born that I haven't been overwhelmed by gratitude for the privilege of being your mother. You both truly are gifts from God.

Forward

This is not just my story. It's not just about how difficult my life was, or the things that happened to me out of my control, or even the poor choices I made that were totally in my control. It's not about whether or not my life was more difficult than someone else's or if I caught better breaks than those around me. It is about the relentless, amazing, abundant love of a God who will do anything to reach all who will give Him a chance.

I struggled tremendously about putting my life experiences out there. Many of them do not show myself or others in a favorable light. I realized, however, as I started to put this book together, that if I did not tell the embarrassing and unfavorable times in my life, the most valuable lessons garnered through these experiences would be lost. And, most importantly, the true impact of how much our God loves us, what He will do for us, and how far He will reach to touch our lives could not be fully realized. Because of that, I know I cannot waste this opportunity God has given me. It is not my intention to dishonor or cause any pain to anyone involved. Having said that, I have changed the names of those involved to protect those that God is still working on.

People close to me, who know a lot of my past, have always told me I should write a book. Although I didn't take it very seriously, that thought was always circling around in my head. Then, one morning during my time in prayer I received a name for a book that was yet to be. I started writing, thinking that I was doing this with the hope of touching people. I also thought, *I am doing this for God – to show what He has done for me*. As I continued to write, however, I slowly began to realize I was doing this for me also.

The majority of my adult life was spent pretending that so much of what I had experienced and had been through did not really happen. I was so sure if people knew, they would think less of me and not like me. I put the memories so far out of my mind that it shocked me when one would rear its ugly head and stir up memories so painful, it seemed as if they had just happened yesterday. I realized healing wasn't going to come by pretending things never happened. This has been a very painful, yet therapeutic journey. The freedom that has come to me by putting this out there is unbelievable.

My prayer is this: whoever picks up and reads this book will be influenced in such a way that his or her life will be changed or that he or she will help to change a life.

This is my testimony...about the amazing, abundant grace of our Lord and Savior, Jesus.

Chapter 1

"Even though I walk through the darkest valley, I will fear no evil, for you are with me; your rod and your staff, they comfort me. You prepare a table before me in the presence of my enemies" (Psalm 23:4-5).

The noise and commotion outside my husband's ICCU room is evidence of a normal workday. Nurses are running here and there, doctor's names are called out over the intercom, and gurneys bring new patients in and the lucky ones out to other floors. Inside my husband's room, it's a different story. The constant beeping of the machines he's hooked up to, the slow methodical sound of the ventilator that is breathing for him, and the medicinal smell all remind me of where I am, but everything seems so surreal. The days go by so quickly, while I sit here not capable of doing anything but thinking and praying and watching for a glimpse of improvement. It's as if I am in a time warp, his room a black hole. It's like an old science fiction movie I've seen where someone is sucked in and separated from the outside world with no way back to normalcy. If I ever thought they didn't exist, my opinion has changed now. Regular life goes on outside my little black hole. People leave and come to work, make dinner plans, and talk about the coming weekend festivities, but that is not my reality anymore. I don't know if it will ever be again.

There are so many thoughts going through my mind right now. I know God always hears me. I know that his plans for me are good. I have seen him do so many amazing things in my life. This? This is a hard one, though. I had prayed so many times for God to deliver David from his addiction and from causing us so much pain. How many times had I prayed, "Father make him stop, help him to stop, but if not take him home. Just stop him from hurting us anymore". Did I really believe that it would end like this? Did I want it to end this way? Was this my fault for not having enough faith that he would be delivered? No, I knew God could do it, that He wanted to do it. It's just that watching him slowly destroy himself and our family over the years made the possibility of it hard to grasp.

Sitting in this sterile room, I feel numb as if I am just floating. This must be the shock that you hear people speak of whenever something traumatic happens. But wait. Where was this underlying peace coming from? It felt so strange, as if I should be more upset. My world is completely turned upside down yet I don't feel disoriented. I feel as if I am literally being held.

In order to understand how huge of a deal this is, you need to understand how I handle emergency situations. Not well, to say the least. It is almost as if I detach from my body and am not able to make any conscious decisions for myself. Instead, I go into an autopilot-like state. In crisis, I carry on with my daily routine, not able to deviate from it. For example, when my father had a sudden stroke, I was told to get to the hospital quickly. What did I do? I took a shower, washed my hair, got dressed, put my makeup on, and continued with my normal routine, not because I wanted to, but because my mind shut down. It went into some kind of protection mode. I could not comprehend the situation I was facing, it did not make sense, and so it could not be happening. That's why, for me, the bizarre calmness that surrounds me is very uncharacteristic.

I had no idea how I would handle things if David didn't make it. On the other hand, I didn't know how I would handle things if he did. How far would he come? Would he be able to take care of himself? And if he couldn't, there sure wasn't any money to provide proper long-term care. Then there was the most important concern of all, my children's faith. They were grown now. They had lived through all of the hard times. Although they had the emotional scars and consequences of living in an abusive, alcoholic, home, they had seen my faith in action. They had seen our God provide over and over. They turned out great because God heard my prayers and was the father their own father hadn't been. In spite of all their father's problems they loved him and he loved them. If he didn't pull through, would they still believe in God and his healing power? Everything was on the line.

I constantly questioned my decision to stay with my husband. I didn't think I had any other choices. I had no money and no job. I had no family to go home to. My mother had made sure I knew that. "There are shelters that will take you and the kids," she'd say. Besides, every time I would pray and tell God I couldn't do it anymore and find the courage to leave, something would always happen. David would either apologize and promise me the world, or just start slowing down the drinking and be home more with us. Thus, my rollercoaster life continued.

This became a ride that sickened me and I couldn't take the motion sickness anymore. I wanted off, like a young child who decides slightly too late that the big kid ride might be just a bit too scary. I was finally finished. I couldn't do it anymore. I had to leave. It had been years and years and I had stuck it out for so long. David's health was deteriorating quickly along with his relationships with all of us. I finally told the Lord, "If you want this family together, YOU will have to do something because I am done." I was just so tired. I had finally come to the end of me. There was no more strength to continue. It is only looking back that I can imagine God saying, "Finally, now I can do something. You finally let go."

We had just recently been inspired by our church to read a book called *The Circle Maker*. The book challenged us to draw imaginary lines around areas of our lives that needed a breakthrough, to pray and fast, and expect God to hear and move. I did just that. I surrounded my family, husband, and marriage in prayer. I fasted for the week and took my lunch hours at work to go to a quiet place and study the Bible and pray. My daughter and son joined me in this. They circled our family and their father. The last day of the fast was the day my husband admitted himself into the hospital. He wasn't feeling well. He was swollen with water from a heart condition made worse by his drinking. He couldn't breathe lying down so he had to sleep the night before sitting up. He knew they would have to detox him first before treating the condition and said he was prepared for this. He said he was ready to quit. I could see the hope in my children's faces. For the first time in a long time, I was hopeful. That hope would quickly transform into one of the most challenging times in the life of my family.

Chapter 2

"Day and night I cry, and tears are my only food... My heart breaks when I remember the past... Why am I so sad? Why am I so troubled? I will put my hope in God, and once again I will praise him, my savior and my God..." **(Psalm 42:3-11).**

My early childhood memories are mixed. There are good ones of long, lazy summer days that seemed to last forever. We practically lived on the beach. We would go down around nine in the morning and stay until evening. Sometimes my father would join us after work and take us out in the water farther than we were able to go ourselves. I also have wonderful memories of summer clambakes. In mid-July, I can remember lying in bed, just having woken up, and hearing the locusts announce the beginning of a hot summer day. I could smell the sweet pungent smell of mulberries from the tree outside my window that had fallen on the ground and started to decay. I would quickly dress and eat and run outside to watch my father prepare for the cookout. He would dig the hole that he would later cook the clams in. He set up the tables and prepared the huge ice buckets that would hold and keep cold the beverages for the day. Time seemed to move very slowly as I waited anxiously for my cousins to arrive.

As fall approached and the holidays neared, I remember having such a sense of excitement. The holiday dinners were usually at our house or my grandmother's. We very seldom saw my father's relatives. My grandmother and mother were good cooks and excellent bakers. I remember, as all the preparation would begin, we made chains to mark down the number of days before Christmas and my excitement would grow as the chain decreased. The day before Christmas my father would take us to get the tree and when we got home we would string the popcorn to decorate it. In addition to those special occasions, my father would take me with him to look at the jobs he was working on. He was a mason, and to this day, the smell of a new house with its fresh wood is one of my favorite smells, along with the salty sea air of the beach.

In addition to these good memories, I also remember being very fearful. From very early on, in fact as far back as I can remember, I have memories of being afraid and not feeling secure. In all of these memories, I have trouble recalling fond ones of my mother. I loved my mother, but it wouldn't become obvious to me until much later in life why I felt the way I did. I have memories of her, but they are not ones of warmth and nurturing. She was physically there, but emotionally absent. It was as if a light switch had been turned off and she wasn't able to show affection. I have no memories of laughing with her, heart-to-heart talks, or hugs. She did things for me. I always had what I needed, physically anyway. She was also very strict when it came to the house. It was immaculate. She always had meals prepared and she baked for us. There were gifts on birthdays and the holidays. Yet, there was a closeness lacking, a connection that I longed for, but was missing. I don't remember ever sitting with her and just talking. I don't remember any one-on-one time with her. There was something missing. I knew it, but I knew nothing else. A strange emptiness lived inside me. To the outside world, it seemed the perfect family. It was exactly how she wanted it to look. Inwardly, I was crying out for help.

Around my 13th birthday, something happened to me. I was a shy child, fearful and easily startled, but there wasn't any indication there was anything wrong with me or with my family. My mother always said I had the best family one could ever hope for. She said we didn't have to tell each other "I love you" or express it. She said it was a given. She couldn't stand when other people showed outward affection in public. She also didn't believe in hugging or showing affection to a child after puberty. Come to think of it, I don't ever remember being told I was loved, or I was good or pretty or that I could do anything I put my mind to. I always felt so empty and couldn't understand where this great love and support was, I certainly hadn't experienced it.

It was at this time that the anxiety set in and it was debilitating. I would find out later that it was part genetic and part environmental. I would also find out years later that my mother suffered from a similar condition, explaining many things I wondered about her as I was growing up. Life became unbearable. I wasn't able to eat, sleep, or concentrate on anything. Thoughts were always racing around in my head, thoughts that were fearful and irrational. No one understood. They took me to doctors who performed blood tests, a spinal tap, etc., but nothing ever showed anything. I remember they prescribed these huge vitamin pills.

At this time they didn't have the medications we have today. Finally, out of desperation, I was prescribed shock treatments, a horror in itself.

I can still remember sitting in the waiting room of the hospital for them to call me in for the treatment. I remember thinking while all my friends at school were sitting in homeroom, I was sitting in the psychiatric ward of the hospital waiting for shocks of electricity to be sent through my brain. I was anxious, yes, I had trouble sleeping and concentrating, but this seemed wrong to me. I knew something was wrong, but, as young as I was, I knew I wasn't crazy. When they called me, they took me into this room and strapped me to a table. They then gave me an injection to put me out and I couldn't remember anything else until I was walking out of the hospital. I needed my mother and grandmother to help me walk out because the anesthesia lingered causing me to be groggy. One particular time, when I went in for a treatment, they must not have put me out deep enough. I can remember feeling this very bad pain shooting in my head. After that, I remember crying and telling them I didn't want to go anymore. The treatments didn't do anything for me. I would feel calmer until the anesthesia wore off and then it was just as if nothing had happened.

I don't recall a lot of the details of this time in my life, either because of the condition itself, the shock treatments, or maybe I just blocked it out of my mind subconsciously. I do know I was taken and left at two different hospitals for evaluation. One of the places was more like a hotel. I remember another young girl a few years older than me, sleeping, always sleeping, with Jimi Hendrix and Black Sabbath music blasting out of her ear phones. I met this young guy there and we hung out together and would talk for hours. I formed strong attachments to different people, always looking for attention and approval. There were no tests performed, no medications given to me. I had appointments with doctors, but all we ever did was talk. I was so tired of talking, of telling them the same things over and over. Then one of the doctors wanted to try to hypnotize me. It didn't work, at least I didn't think it did. After that, he told my parents to take me home. "Let her get back to school and her life."

Apparently, I wasn't fixed yet so my parents placed me in another hospital. This one was a state hospital, dark and dingy, different than the other. There were other children there with serious emotional problems. I remember being so afraid, especially of one boy, who even the nurses and orderlies had trouble controlling. My mother said they didn't have the money to keep me in the nicer place. I remember being left there by my parents, my eyes filling with tears, begging them not to leave me there. I wanted to go home. I didn't know why I couldn't. I didn't understand why they didn't want me home. I wasn't a problem to anyone and it wasn't my fault I didn't feel good. What I do know is that I was very young, afraid, and alone. I was 14 years old. I remember lying down on a cot in an empty, sterile room and just crying myself to sleep. I felt so alone and abandoned. No one came to visit me. Finally, after a month, a doctor who had been treating me told my parents to take me home and let me get back to as normal a life routine as possible. He said that I didn't belong there. Why was I there in the first place? Why couldn't they find someone on an outpatient basis to treat me? Why didn't they care enough to keep me?

I was finally back home. I tried to act as if everything was fine. I hid, as well as I could, the thoughts and feelings I didn't understand from everyone so as not to be sent away again. I tried so very hard to pretend that everything was okay. What I didn't understand at that time is that I had a condition known as Obsessive Compulsive Disorder. They didn't know much about this condition back then and it was something not talked about. I always had very good grades in school, so I knew I was smart. I learned quickly. Others would tell me how pretty I was. "Why don't you do this or do that?" But it didn't matter, because I was a mess on the inside.

Although I don't recall a lot of details about this time, I do remember that my whole outlook on life began to change from this point on. I began to become resentful and rebellious. I had serious abandonment issues because of what I had experienced. I developed a mindset that I would do what it took to survive, no matter what. I didn't trust anyone and felt that I couldn't let people know anything about me. I felt that I was an embarrassment and if people knew the real me they wouldn't like me. I also felt so alone. I needed to feel some form of love or acceptance and began to make choices that would affect the rest of my life.

We attended an Episcopalian church. They believed in God the Father, Jesus Christ, and the Holy Spirit. I attended Catechism classes and I was confirmed. We had the stations-of-the-cross and sermons that were long and boring and we had to stand up and sit down and cross ourselves and repeat prayers from a book. Everyone did and said the same thing. People came in and went out the same way they came. God seemed so distant and far off. I had no idea what Jesus had actually done for us during his crucifixion and resurrection. I had no idea that I could have a relationship with this Jesus and that he had provided healing and an abundant life for me.

One Sunday morning I was sitting in church, looking up at the huge crucifix overhead, wondering who this God really was. I remembered a few years ago a family in the church had a little baby that died of some terrible disease. I was younger and not involved in the conversation, standing alongside my mother, listening to the other women talking, saying how it was God's will that it happened. Really, this God of love wanted this little baby to die like that? Where was this love they were always talking about? They said God was love, right? Leaving the church, a sick, empty feeling engulfed me. Yet, underneath the emptiness, there was something else. I felt a tugging at my heart. There had to be more than this. There had to be a reason for us being here. Were we just put here to suffer and then die? That seemed like a cruel joke. I wanted to know this God, but I was afraid. What if what those women said was right? If that was His will, I certainly didn't want it in my life.

Chapter 3

"Have I not commanded you? Be strong and courageous. Do not be terrified; do not be discouraged, for the LORD your God will be with you wherever you go" (Joshua 1:9).

D avid had been in the hospital three days. They were giving him medication to help with the alcohol withdrawal. We had just visited with him the day before and he was sitting up talking with us, but overnight everything changed.

I had been at the hospital all day and was tired. The nurse is evasive and clearly has no answers to my questions. There hasn't been a doctor in to see my husband in spite of the ten or so times I have asked for one. When my daughter, Tia, walks in she is visibly upset by what is going on. Tia asks the same questions I have asked all day with no answers. "Why is he so agitated? Why is his breathing so labored? Is it normal for him to go in and out of consciousness?" They sent in an ENT to evaluate him, only to find out that when they tried to wake him he was too agitated to answer any questions and could not be evaluated. They ask me if he has sleep apnea, which he does, but even I can tell that isn't the issue here. Finally, they send in a nurse practitioner, not the doctor who should have been overseeing his case. The nurse decides that because he is so agitated and seems to be worsening, they are going to increase his Ativan to every hour on the hour. She proceeds to ask me if I agree with her. I wonder, *how am I supposed to make this type of decision?* I told her if that was what they thought, then yes. By this time both Tia's and my nerves are completely on edge. Our exhaustion and aggravation lead to us arguing because she feels I should stay the night when all I want to do is go home and lie down.

Rushing out of the hospital room to pick-up my grandsons from school, Tia leaves me frustrated, feeling that I need to do more. As early evening comes around, exhaustion wins and I leave to go home, get something to eat, and rest. I drop on the couch, wanting desperately to relax when all I can do is relive the day's events. David's breathing progressively worsened over the course of the day, and up until the time I left, no doctor had been in to evaluate his condition or listen to my concerns. He was in and out of consciousness, mostly out, and when he was conscious he was extremely agitated and made no sense. "They don't know what they are doing, "he yelled. To my horror, I would find out later that he made perfect sense. They, in fact, did not know what they were doing.

I knew alcohol withdrawal could be tough. Although the couple of times before, when I had watched David go through it, it wasn't anything like this. One time, years before, David had a close encounter with overdosing on alcohol and pills and was rushed to the hospital. After spending three days in the psychiatric ward, he came home. I asked to have a couple of my close friends from church come and pray with him. David woke up the next day and was completely delivered from his addiction. He still wasn't at the place where he understood what was done for him. He took up walking and started taking care of himself. We were all so excited. Still, I saw behavior in him that caused me to be concerned. He still didn't go to church on a regular basis. He didn't have any fellowship with other believers and I never saw him read the Bible or pray. There's a passage in scripture where Jesus heals a man and tells him to change his behavior and seek God in all that he does lest something worse happens to him. I was trying not to be negative, but I knew in my heart he was still trying to do it all on his own. He was sober for almost four months before he began drinking again.

Having been through so many life-threatening scenarios with David in the past, whether out of neglect or just plain stupid decision making, I knew he always pulled through. I was becoming used to it even though I am aware of how terribly strange that sounds. How can someone get used to this? There was the time he was shot in his head because of a bad business decision and being in the wrong place at the wrong time. I received the call at 1:00 in the morning to come immediately. They didn't know if he would make it through the night. Or there was the time he and a few of his friends were stuck out on his boat. They were in the canyon for three days, stuck in a storm that came out of nowhere. Even the Coast Guard couldn't help him out of that one. I honestly felt this was just another one of those times. I was tired and fed up with his drinking and if this is what it took, then so be it. He had done this to himself.

Sensing that something was terribly wrong, Tia returned that evening after her husband came home to watch their boys. As she sat there watching her father and the machines measuring his vital signs, her older brother, my stepson, David walked into the room. Together, they sat there agreeing that their father's breathing seemed to be worsening and that they needed to speak with a doctor.

I jumped almost off the couch with the shrill ring of the phone. I heard my daughter on the other end anxiously spewing out questions and statements. "They want to know if dad has a living will." "Why are they asking for that now?" "His breathing is really not good now, mom." "Maybe you should come back here and stay the night with him."

I told Tia I would get off of the phone with her and call the nurse and see what was going on. I got the nurse manager on the phone and as she started to explain his condition, I heard commotion in the background. Then I heard the nurse I was talking to yell, "Oh my God!" followed by the phone sounding like it had been dropped. I heard, "Code blue! Code blue!" and people running in the background. I started to shake, not sure of what I had just heard, if it was about David or not. I hung up the phone, shaking, not sure what my next move should be. Immediately the phone rings and I hear Tia's voice, "Mom, get here now!" And just like that, she's gone.

My inability to handle emergency situations kicks in. I zone out. Not quite sure what to do first, I yell to Jacob, "We have to go to the hospital. Something bad is happening and I don't know what's going on." I try to find clothes to put on, but can't and finally drag something out of the hamper. Forget the make-up or the hair. I had to find my pocketbook and couldn't remember where I had put it. Jacob yells, "Mom, forget it and just get in the car!" He drives like a crazy person, passing everyone and running every light. My mind and heart race and the words won't come to pray so I pray in the spirit. We jump out of the car without parking it and start to run. I had injured my foot and was in a boot, so I couldn't move fast. Hobbling down the endless corridor to the elevator, I yell repeatedly for Jacob to wait for me. As we approach the waiting area on his floor, I hug Tia and David as they fill me in on what happened.

David's breathing had been very labored and Tia, watching him exhale, looked to make sure his vitals were okay. After what seemed an eternity she jumped up and shouted, "He's not breathing!" The aide next to the bed said, "He's fine. He is still registering on the machine." Then David jumped up and yelled, "No, he's not! He's not breathing!" David ran into the hallway screaming for help. Nurses, aides, and doctors all came running into the room. Tia and David were pushed outside and slid down onto the floor, holding onto each other. His heart had stopped and they worked furiously to revive him. They finally got his heart to start beating, but it had taken twelve minutes. Twelve minutes! No one could tell us what had happened to him during those twelve minutes. Was that too long of a time? Would there be brain damage? He was in a coma. Would he ever come out of the coma?

He was now stable, but critical and they were still working on him so we wait for what seems like an eternity in the waiting area. Our close friends from church come, our pastor comes, David's older, estranged daughter comes with her two children, who are 14 and 12 years old. Around one o'clock in the morning, they wheel him into the elevator to take him to the ICCU where we will wait for the next three weeks, not knowing if he will survive or how much he will recover.

My daughter, Tia, and my son, Jacob, were angry. Tia told me, "Mom, God could have taken him at any time before this and I would've understood. But for God to take him now after all the prayers and fasting, when he actually came here for help, I don't understand, and honestly my faith is going to be seriously affected if he dies like this or stays in a coma. I just wanted a few years with my father as my father." Jacob was feeling the same way, and had more questions than faith at this point. All I could pray at this point was, "I know how David lived and I accept whatever the outcome, but please don't let my children lose their faith."

Chapter 4

"You are my refuge, my portion in the land of the living." Listen to my cry, for I am in desperate need; rescue me from those who pursue me, for they are too strong for me. Set me free from my prison, that I may praise your name. Then the righteous will gather about me because of your goodness to me" **(Psalm 142:5-7).**

I was so confused and unhappy. There were times when thoughts would come in my mind like…*You can just end it all now and then you wouldn't have to struggle like this anymore.* Or…*It's never going to get any better, you know that.* And especially…*They don't really love you anyway.* I would push the thoughts out and attempt to pull myself together. It was a struggle to do the normal things kids did. I was desperate to feel loved and understood, but all I felt was different and scared. I went back and forth between moments of despair and a strong, overwhelming desire to overcome and survive. Where this will to survive came from I wasn't sure, but it was a driving force. I would look back years later and realize that those moments of strength came only from God. I didn't know God at this point in my life, but He knew me. In His infinite wisdom, He knew the plans He had for me. His plans were to give me a hope and a future. His plans were for good and not for evil.

I, on the other hand, couldn't see His plans. There was so much I didn't understand. One day out of desperation and anger I went to the library and took out books on witchcraft. I tried casting spells. I wanted answers to my pain and I tried to get those answers without consulting the One who had all the answers. This period of rebellion didn't last long, but it was enough to open the door to all kinds of guilt. It gave evil a foothold in my life. My interest in witchcraft died as quickly as it began, but a period of rebellion opened up that led me down a road of more suffering and pain. I know now that could have been avoided, if only someone had been there to teach me and instruct me in the ways of God.

It was the summer of 1969. I was 15 years old. It was the year of Woodstock, a time of great questioning, rebellion, and experimenting. Drugs were rampant, sex was breaking free from the confines of our parents' generation, and war was in full swing in Vietnam. Adding all of that together with my own confusion and suffering equaled a real mess! I couldn't concentrate enough to get through a day of school, never mind my sophomore year of high school. So I quit. I just walked out. My parents were beside themselves. "What would people think?" *Did they really think I cared?* I didn't know how to help myself.

The friends that I hung out with were older. Some had moved out of their parents homes and rented rooms in buildings down by the beach. We hung out and listened to Janice Joplin and Jimi Hendrix. It would be fair to say that surfing was the main sport in our little beach community, except I think it took second place to the drugs of that time. We spent our days hanging out in dark and dingy small rooms with clouds of sweet pungent smoke swirling around us. Time quickly slipped away as we discussed the problems our country was facing and how our generation was going to be so different. We would never conform to society's ideals. Every evening we would all gather down by the beach at a small deli called Johnny's. There was a pinball machine and foosball game in the back, behind the tables. The draft had been instituted and many of the older boys were being called to serve. Some left for Canada, while others went on drug binges for weeks before reporting in, in the hopes of failing their physicals.

My parent's reactions to the choices I was making were anger and frustration. They had trouble controlling me. I was told if I didn't go back to school, I had to go to work. What they didn't realize is that I wasn't trying to hurt them, I was just hurting so badly myself. I couldn't handle the anxiety and the deep-seated feeling of despair. I needed help and it seemed as if no one cared. I finally got a job in a factory. They made parts for radios and televisions. My job was to look through a machine that looked like a microscope and line up certain pieces. It was a boring job and not something I wanted to do for very long, never mind the rest of my life.

I also threw myself into a relationship with a boy I should never have been seeing. His main source of income was selling drugs. Because he was a dealer, I had access to just about any type of drug I wanted. I experimented with all different kinds of drugs in an effort to ease the pain I felt. I would get home from work and go out and not come back until the early morning hours. Sometimes I wouldn't come home at all. I had an older friend who rented a room down by the ocean for a week. She asked if I would come and stay with her. I told my father what I was planning on doing. I still remember thinking that I really didn't want to go. I thought for sure he would tell me I couldn't. He looked right at me and said, "Fine, just don't' come home pregnant." I didn't realize at the time how out of control my life was. I was looking for a way, any way, to end the pain and to feel loved and wanted. Instead, at fifteen years old, I ended up pregnant.

My mother made an appointment with a hospital in New York where abortions were legal. Without even considering any input from me, I was told I was going there the following morning. I was scheduled to have the baby aborted. Hardly old enough to comprehend what was about to happen, I had this horrible sick, guilty feeling that my whole world was spinning out of control. No one sat me down and talked to me. No one asked me what I was thinking, or what I wanted. Shame hung over me and our house like a black cloud. Nothing much was said. It would have been so much better if there had been some type of emotional display. I felt I wasn't even worth that. There was no talk of God. There were no prayers said in my home that I was aware of or that I heard. And there was certainly not one mention of the sin that aborting a baby was. My mother had always taken us to church when we were young. We never discussed God outside of church though. Today, I understand that she could not give me what she didn't have herself.

The following morning I heard the rain falling outside my windows. Today was the day my father was taking me to the hospital and leaving me there until all was over and done. I was five months pregnant. The procedure to abort a five month fetus involved actual labor and delivery. I was terrified. I also felt an enormous amount of regret, for what I had done and what I was about to do to an innocent baby. I was so mixed up and frightened. I don't remember my mother saying anything to me that morning. I packed up a few items and got into the car with my father. My father was a very quiet man. He drank a lot, but was never abusive. His father had been an alcoholic and he had had a tough upbringing. I loved my father very much, even though he wasn't very verbal or sensitive. He didn't hug me, but I knew he loved me. He was the one I would talk with about things. Today was different. There was nothing to be said. He was the one who took me to the hospital, not my mother. I think he just didn't know how to express himself.

It was now drizzling, dreary, and very grey. The ride seemed endless and yet I didn't want it to end because I knew my father would be leaving me. We went to admissions, I was given a room, and my father left. I watched him walk out, once more leaving me alone, afraid, and confused. I desperately needed someone to hold me and tell me it was going to be okay.

A little while later, in the early afternoon, the doctor and nurse came in and had me prepped. They explained that I would be receiving an injection in my uterus, a saline mixture of some sort, to start my contractions and cause me to go into labor. They could not tell me how long this would take. "Everyone is different." Well into the late evening, I was lying in bed and couldn't sleep. I could hear screams coming from down the hall. The piercing screams were later identified to me as a twelve-year-old girl in labor. There was no one to talk to. Thoughts that terrified me raced around in my head. *Why was my life such a mess? Wasn't there anyone who really cared what happened to me? Was I really that difficult to love?* In the middle of the night I remember having what I thought were bad gas pains. I thought maybe the dinner they had given me was making me sick. Finally, I called for the nurse and she explained that labor had started. She checked me and said she would come back in an hour to check on me again. Early in the morning hours, they wheeled me into a delivery room where I delivered a baby. They never told me what it was and I never saw it. I never felt so alone. I cried myself to sleep.

The following morning when I couldn't get a hold of my parents to tell them that I wanted to come home, I finally called my aunt. I spoke to her briefly, asking if she knew where my mother was. She asked me where I was and I proceeded to explain where I was and why, never stopping to think that my mother would be upset if I told someone else where I was or what was going on. Finally, my father came to pick me up. I was an emotional mess because of my hormones and I was extremely upset with the lack of feeling or support from my parents, especially my mother. When we finally pulled into the driveway, my mother met me at the door. She wasn't greeting me to see how I was, but to let me know that I had no business telling my aunt what was going on and to stop walking "that way" or the neighbors would know what had happened. I felt completely alone, unloved, embarrassed, ashamed, and consumed in guilt. I slipped into my bed and cried myself to sleep again.

Chapter 5

"For the Son of Man came to seek and to save that which was lost" (Luke 19:10).

At the same time my life was falling apart with no apparent help in sight, a "Jesus movement" was underway. Hanging out in a small town down by the ocean one evening, I was approached by some young adults with pamphlets about Jesus. Sure, growing up in an Episcopalian church, I knew about Jesus, but I had never heard anything like what these people were saying about him. He loved me. *Me? The unlovable? He cares what happens to me?* They had my attention.

There were tent revival meetings going on and kids from all over the area were attending. I was swept up in the revival and for the first time I could remember, I had a reason to live and a direction to go in. There were Sunday morning services, Sunday evening services, and also a Wednesday evening service. I attended them all regularly. They held a baptism service at the end of that summer and I was baptized in a river. I was so excited about being baptized that I invited my parents to come. To my surprise they came. It was years later that my father told me at the time he was thinking, "What is my crazy daughter doing now?" What neither of us knew at the time was that it was planting seeds in my father that would later be used to bring him to salvation. It was an overcast, chilly day in November and the water was frigid, but none of us involved paid attention to the environment. I heard some of those who were attending, and not participating, saying we were insane and that we would all get sick. Amazingly, not one of us did.

This was my first introduction to the beautiful, amazing grace of Jesus Christ. I really didn't understand a lot at this time, but I just knew that I wanted to know more and more about this Jesus and his love for me. I was so on fire with his love that I just had to tell everyone I met and, thinking back, I did. We went to the boardwalk and handed out fliers to anyone who passed by. We had Bible studies during the week at friends' houses. I just wanted to get as much of this Jesus as I could, the beginning of a whole new world had been opened up for me.

I knew very little about spiritual warfare at this time. I just knew that there was a God and He loved me. I know many people laugh at the thought that we have an enemy, but oh how we do! What happened next in my life changed its direction for a while. Although I may not know until I get to Heaven why things happened the way they did, I do know that God turns the plans of evil into good for those who trust him, even when it isn't immediately apparent. I was so excited with my new outlook on life. Things weren't perfect but I had reason to believe they would only get better. I was reading my bible and making new friends. The anxiety I suffered from was still a daily part of my life, but I was functioning better than I had in a long time. I was sleeping better and I started to put on some much needed weight. My hair started to grow again and I looked healthier than I had in a long time. My new friends were older and getting ready to graduate high school and go off to a bible college. One summer evening we went over to our pastor's house to discuss Bible college options for them. I was upset realizing that they would be leaving me soon. I hadn't finished high school, so I was in no position to join them. I was feeling confused about where my life was headed and wishing I could go off with my friends to bible college. I waited until the end of the evening and asked the pastor if I could speak with him. I'm not sure what I wanted him to tell me. I couldn't talk to anyone at home, especially about this. They didn't understand. I was hoping he would have some advice as to how to get my life back on track. We were in his home and his wife and five children where there also. I had no reason to believe anything could or would possibly go wrong. He took me outside and we started walking and as I started to explain my problem, he suddenly stopped me. He grabbed me by the arm, pulled me in, and started to kiss me. At first I was confused. I was only sixteen and he was well over forty. I had no attraction to him and no idea that anything like that was on his mind. As he continued to pull me tighter, I pushed back, and ran away. I ran all the way back to the house before I realized the tears that were sliding down my checks. I was shaking and the confusion I felt quickly turned to anger. *Why? What just happened? What had I done wrong?* Once again, my whole world turned upside down. *Was this whole thing about Jesus just someone's cruel idea of a joke?* I never went back to that church. In fact, I didn't bother going to church at all. The pastor actually had a letter sent to my house. How could I leave the church with all they had done for me?" I am sure now that he was afraid of what I may say and was trying to protect himself. If he knew how beaten down I was, he could have saved himself the time and cost of the postage. I just felt like I got what was coming to me and deserved no better. I didn't find out until years later that he had done this to other women in the church as well.

An Abundance of Grace

Had this not happened to me I don't know the direction my life may have taken. Maybe I could have avoided a lot of pain and heartache, but I have to believe there was a reason and that God brought something good out of that situation. I still had this deep desire to know Jesus, but I was confused and angry. My emotions were so conflicting. Looking back, I realize Jesus never left me, even during the years following when I slipped back into rebellion.

I may have turned and run away from the Lord, but he certainly didn't turn from me. He kept pursuing me. My anxiety was less severe and I could function. This was nothing short of a miracle. I went back to high school. I was two years behind my classmates so I doubled up on my classes. When it came time for my classmates to graduate, I was still short credits. My brother was a year behind me and this meant I would have to graduate with his class and I couldn't bring myself to do that. So, once again I quit. This time though, I went to work during the day and took classes at night in order to graduate, which I did. I went on to business school and graduated from there also. I was busy pushing myself, so I didn't have to think about the past. Funny thing is, once the Lord gets a hold of you he doesn't let go. You can run from Him, but He is still always with you and doesn't give up on you.

I applied for a model/waitress job up at Newark Airport, which I got, and packed-up my stuff and moved there. I wanted out of my house. I wanted to be as far away as possible from everything I knew and had been through. Once I moved up north, a whole new world opened up to me. It was definitely not where I should have been, but at least I wasn't surrounded by my past. I was living on my own. First, I was in a hotel where my job put me up. Then, I rented an apartment with a friend I met at work and we started partying and drinking…a lot. The men that frequented my job had all types of "offers." There were several offers to model at some well-known establishments, offers for jobs that would require me to travel out of state with some of these men, offers to work private parties, and offers from those who just wanted to go out and party. The attention was overwhelming. It was like the world had sent out these huge tentacles in an effort to grab me and pull me in deeper than I already was. As much as I enjoyed the attention, I was afraid and very cautious. Something kept me from accepting most of the offers. I think deep inside I knew if I followed those routes, I wouldn't make it. I wasn't strong enough.

Still searching for love and acceptance, I reached out the only way I knew. I became involved with a young man. I wouldn't just start dating someone, I would throw myself completely into the relationship, mentally as well as physically. The thing is when you don't address your problems and run from them, they always have a way of catching up to you and you end up repeating your past. I became pregnant again. I wanted to get married and have the baby. The guy I was dating was just not ready for anything like that. After weeks of crying and pleading, I resigned myself to the idea of another abortion. I certainly couldn't go home. The words of my parents still resounded in my mind, "Don't come home pregnant." At this point in my life, I was fully aware of the sin of aborting a child, but I was so hurt and felt so abandoned by everyone that I just didn't see any other way out. I didn't have the emotional strength to try and find other help. I honestly didn't think it existed. No one really cared. At this point in my life, I was still running away from God and still afraid of what His will for me was. Had I only known then what I know now, that His will is the best plan for me, I could have saved myself so much heart ache, pain, and remorse. The emotional turmoil was so great and I was exhausted. I had a second abortion. I knew God was forgiving, so I asked Jesus to forgive me before I did it, but I was pretty sure it didn't work that way and that He didn't care either. This forgiveness couldn't be for someone who had done what I had. I never got mad at God. I never thought He didn't exist. I didn't shake my fists at Him. Deep inside I felt that He couldn't love me. I didn't know how to receive the love He had for me. I was beaten down by life, figured it had to be my fault, and had only just turned 19 years old.

I knew I couldn't go home. My mother didn't want me back, that was for sure. I had no idea what to do. When you don't think clearly, don't consult the Lord as to what steps you need to take, and make all of your decisions on your own, chances are you're headed for trouble. And that is exactly where I was at…headed for more trouble.

Chapter 6

"Peace I leave with you; my peace I give you. I do not give to you as the world gives. Do not let your hearts be troubled and do not be afraid" (John 14:27).

The ICCU floor had a strange set up. The nurse's station was in the center as if the patient rooms orbited around it. It kind of made sense when I thought about it. Just like the Earth revolves around the sun and life on this planet depends on the sun, the life of those patients depended on the nurses and doctors that inhabited that station. These people would not be alive except for extreme medical intervention. Walking down the corridor on the opposite side of the ICCU floor, I could look across the nurse's station and see into my husband's room. He laid there, motionless, tubes of all sorts connected to him. There was a machine that was breathing for him and others keeping track of his vital signs. I walked in and put down my purse and water. *Oh, David what have you done?* All the anger melted out of me. He looked just as helpless as I felt. I didn't know if he would ever open his eyes again. I didn't know if he would ever speak or laugh or see his children again. I felt sorry for him. I think it was there that I began to realize the power of the addiction that had him so bound.

For the next three weeks I went and spent as much time as I could in that room with David. Although my immediate boss at the time had told me to take whatever time I needed to be there for my husband, the Human Resources Department did not share that opinion. They wanted me to use whatever sick or vacation time I had accrued. The problem with that was I had no idea how long this would go on and I had a limited amount of time. I had to settle for going there on my lunch hour and after work. Between my daughter, my son, and myself, we tried to have someone there as much as possible to keep an eye on what was going on. He was on a different floor now, but still in the same hospital that had just over-prescribed medication for him and almost killed him. His heart stopped, we later learned, because he had been given too much Ativan. *David, you were right. They didn't know what they were doing.* We weren't about to let that happen again. I sat there and watched him for any type of progress; for the slightest movement that meant there was enough brain activity for him to come out of the coma. I watched as they rolled him over and repositioned him to prevent bedsores. I listened to the horrific sound as they suctioned out his breathing tube.

We were always asking for progress reports. "What are his chances?" And we always received the same answer, "There's no way to tell." He went into pneumonia and came down with a bladder infection. We learned the numbers they wanted to see on the breathing machine that would mean they may be able to start to take the tube out, so we diligently watched the numbers go up and then back down. I began to know my way around the hospital and the names of the doctors and nurses and their shift times. I felt as if I was in limbo. I didn't want to be there, but I couldn't be anywhere else. All the hurt and anger I had felt because of the way David had treated us was being replaced with a feeling of sympathy. I felt the need to protect him. He hadn't died.

God had kept him alive for a reason and I was sure it wasn't to lie in a vegetative state for the rest of his life.

I have found that it's always in my darkest moments that God's grace and power shines the brightest. It is when I reach the point of realizing there's nothing I can do, that I'm not in control, that I finally am able to let go and enter into that place of rest I was created to dwell in. We need to reside in that place continually, but I had yet to reach the place in my walk where I had learned to do that. I was now learning firsthand what that meant, realizing that everything was out of my hands. There wasn't a doctor who could give us any answers. There wasn't a test to be performed that could give us hope. One night my son, sitting in his father's room, so concerned and trying to grasp on to whatever little hope someone could give him, asked his father's nurse what she thought. The woman looked at him and without a hint of compassion told him, "What you see is what you get." That answer must have come from such a dry and dead place inside her. When you have been given the gift of life, you can sense another's lack of it. At first I was angry with the nurse, having made my son to feel so hopeless. Then I felt sad for her, knowing that she must feel as hopeless inside as she sounded to us. It made me press all the more into my faith, into a God that I knew could do anything. Nothing is too difficult for Him and He loves us with an everlasting love and will do whatever it takes to bring us to a point where we reach out to him.

We watched day and night for any sign of improvement. I still remember the first time David opened his eyes, we were so excited, only to learn that it was only a reflex and nothing to be happy about. These random movements and jerks, to the untrained eye, seemed like great improvements. They were, however, nothing more than the outward manifestations of his damaged brain. It amazed me how little the doctors, even the neurologists, knew about how and if the brain can heal itself from this type of trauma. The brain wasn't going to heal on its own. God was going to do it in His timing. We were told to look for him consciously following a command. If that happened, there was a sign of hope.

Jacob, Tia, and I were constantly in a cycle of hope and depression. While we were hopeful and anxiously waiting for God's healing, our human nature took over causing us to stumble into wrong thinking. It was really rough. I remember Tia telling me that one morning she was just crying out to God from a really dark place, angry with what was going on, and God led her to two scriptures in an amazing way. She was tired, emotionally and physically. She didn't know where to begin studying God's Word, but she knew she had to because she needed hope. As she was flipping through the pages, certain passages looked highlighted, so she began to read even though she didn't recognize them at all. From Psalm 107: 17-21 she read, "Some became fools through their rebellious ways and suffered affliction because of their iniquities. They loathed all food and drew near the gates of death. Then they cried to the Lord in their trouble, and he saved them from their distress. He sent out his word and healed them; he rescued them from the grave. Let them give thanks to the Lord for his unfailing love and his wonderful deeds for mankind." She also read Psalm 107: 10-14 which spoke so clearly about David's addiction and his coma. "Some sat in darkness, in utter darkness, prisoners suffering in iron chains, because they rebelled against God's commands and despised the plans of the Most High. So he subjected them to bitter labor; they stumbled, and there was no one to help. Then they cried to the Lord in their trouble, and he saved them from their distress. He brought them out of darkness, the utter darkness, and broke away their chains." Tia called me in tears. She knew God was going to heal her dad. He told her so. When she looked backed to read the scriptures to me over the phone, they were no longer highlighted.

David had been in the ICCU for about 3 weeks and there was no real sign of improvement so far. We felt that God was going to do something but it was so hard waiting. It was just another day, and Tia, Jacob, and I were all visiting David. We were talking to him as we always did, but this time was different. He responded with movement. We then specifically asked him to move his toe if he heard us. His toe slowly moved back and forth. We screamed so loudly that the nurses had to come in and tell us to be quiet. It was our first sign of hope! God was working!

Chapter 7

"And we know that in all things God works for the good of those who love him, who have been called according to his purpose" (Romans 8:28).

It had been four weeks and David was now physically stable, but still in a coma. The hospital said their job was done and we needed to find another place for him to go. Insurance wasn't going to pay for him to stay there any longer. Our problem now was that we wanted him in a place that would give him therapy and help him recover, but most places wouldn't take him because he did not show enough signs of improvement to warrant therapy. One place that specialized in brain injuries and would have been our first choice wouldn't take him because of his history of alcohol abuse. His recovery was skeptical and the insurance company wouldn't pay for him to be there. We were being told at this point that a nursing home would be his only option. The insurance companies were now setting the requirements of where he could go. Their first concern was not where he would get the best treatment, but where would they spend the least amount of money. Once again, we were being told, "What you see is what you get." No one held out any hope for David. After a long day of meetings and fighting with the powers that be, we finally found a rehab facility that would take him and at a 10-minute drive, it was close enough for us to go and visit him. This was an awesome answer to prayer. They put him on the bottom floor which was essentially the nursing home facility. They had rehabilitation on the third floor, but when they evaluated him they said he was not "rehabilitation material." They felt that he would never progress enough to warrant therapy.

David was in what they called a "coma emergence state." He was awake and knew us, but he would go in and out of awareness of his surroundings. He thought we had bought a new home. He would think he was on a job at work, yelling and shouting orders to his employees. He had no idea what year it was and it was as if he was living twenty years in the past. He would see people that weren't there. Tia was visiting her father one day and went to sit in the chair and he yelled out, "Watch out! Don't sit on him." He saw someone sitting in the chair, but no one was there. He would tell me later that he continually saw a dark, faceless figure in a long black robe. He was very agitated most of the time. David would also go through the motions of drinking, lifting a non-existent glass to his mouth which was hard to watch. He wasn't able to lift himself or turn himself in his bed. He had to be lifted by a machine so the aides could change him and clean him up. He wore diapers and was fed by a tube.

Insurance had him evaluated every two weeks in order to see if he made enough improvement for them to continue paying for him. Once the improvements stopped, they would discontinue the coverage at which time I would have to pay for him to stay wherever I could afford to keep him. The problem was I didn't have any money to put him anywhere. I contacted an elder management company to see what my options were. I was concerned about them taking the house. After spending money we couldn't afford to spend, hoping they would tell us something that would help us, they informed me that Medicaid couldn't take my house, but they would be taking 80% of my husband's income. If that was the case, they might as well just take the house, because without his income I wouldn't be able to afford to stay there anyway. Every couple of weeks we anxiously waited to hear what his report would say.

Everything, once again, was so surreal. It was as if everything was spinning out of my control and I was watching it, unable to do anything about it. Yet, I had this peace that passed all my understanding. I just kept praying and telling God everyday my situation. I told him that I had no idea what to do. I prayed for David constantly. My church prayed. My friends prayed. I got up and went to work. I left work to go visit him every night. When I would leave at night, I would feel so bad seeing him lay there in that bed staring at the TV, not knowing if he would ever walk on his own, eat a meal, or be well enough to ever leave that place.

I believe that God is definitely in control of our lives, but there is a part we play in that. There are conditions to the promises of God. He is sovereign, but he made us with a free will. He has rules and laws of faith that he has set up. We all have choices to make. When we make choices that we know go against what God tells us is right, we make problems for ourselves. Many of the things we encounter are because we bring them on ourselves. Yes, we live in a fallen world and there is evil, but our God has given us a whole set of instructions in the Bible, to teach us and guide us and to let us know His will for our lives and how to overcome the evil that exists. With that being said, yes, David was in this place because of the many wrong choices he had made, but now he was in no condition to make any choices and I watched as our God intervened on my husband's behalf. The saying that God will turn what the enemy means for evil into good is so true. David had been through so much, he had lost weight and most of the strength he had was gone. He wasn't even able to drink a glass of water at this time. Not only could he not hold it and bring it to his mouth, but he was not able to swallow the water for fear of it going into his lungs and causing pneumonia. He had been in the nursing home for about two weeks and there was no sign of anyone trying to work with him to rehabilitate him. He needed to be on the third floor for that and the therapists said he didn't qualify to go there. "He won't respond," they said.

All of a sudden, David came down with C-Dif, an infection that causes severe diarrhea. He needed to be quarantined because it is very contagious. Anyone working with him or visiting him would have to wear a gown, gloves, and shoe covers. The infection would keep him confined to his room and visitation would be limited. I was upset thinking this was only going to make him weaker and hinder him from making any progress at all. Once again, a negative report was handed to me. The head nurse on the floor where David was informed me that once they get this infection, it is extremely difficult to get rid of it and basically said it would be downhill from there. By this time, I was finally learning to trust more in the amazing power of my God and I was also learning to stand on His promises. I refused to accept the diagnosis that the nurse gave me and started believing that David would get over this and would get better. I was more determined than ever not to let fear rule my heart.

It turned out that the only place they had available at that time to quarantine him was on the third floor. The third floor!!! They moved David up there and his room was two doors down from the therapy room. Therapy was part of the daily routine on the third floor, so as soon as they got the infection under control they started working with him and he started making progress. He made progress so quickly that even the therapists were surprised. God was turning what seemed to be a set back into a tremendous step forward and it was amazing watching it all unfold.

Chapter 8

"There is a way that appears to be right, but in the end it leads to death. Even in laughter the heart may ache, and rejoicing may end in grief" (Proverb 14:12-14).

One night a man about ten years my senior, came into my job. He owned his own business, had money, and didn't mind spending it. There was a rumor about him circulating among the girls that he had money and was looking for someone to go out with. My interest was piqued and it was no secret he was interested in me. His name was David and he was always hanging around where I was. He was spending a ton of money at the restaurant. He thought nothing of taking all the day shift girls, sixteen to be exact, out for dinner and a night out. I started to realize that I didn't care for the person he was and I began to ignore him. The more I did, the more he pursued me.

I had become so hardened by the things life had thrown at me and the things I had done that I began thinking of ways to protect myself at any cost. I had lost all sensitivity to the Holy Spirit (the little that I had learned in the short time I was in church). I didn't pray anymore. I started to think that even though I knew it would not be a good choice, he could be my way out of my mess. A group of us were invited to his house for a pool party one night. I went with my friend from work. When we got there, we found out he was married with two young children who were away with their mother for the weekend. Even that didn't stop me from being interested. I didn't care at this point.

He had a large English Tudor home in northern New Jersey with an in-ground pool. He drove a Jaguar and his wife drove a Mercedes. The house was extravagantly decorated with antiques and leather furniture. After drinking and partying the whole night, I wasn't in any condition to drive an hour and a half home, so I stayed the night. I got up early and went home the next day. I was considering modeling and had an appointment with a photographer to have pictures taken. David called and asked me to cancel and come back. He said we'd go out. I cancelled my appointment and decided to go with him. As I was on my way back up north, I heard a very clear voice in my mind say, "No!" It wasn't my own thought. I knew that. I had a very good idea that I was being told not to go through with my plans. I may not have been paying attention to God, but he was certainly watching over me. To this day I still remember my reaction to this warning and I cringe. My response was out loud and in a defiant voice. "No, I am going to do this!" This one decision made in rebellion is definitely one I would come to regret. Even when God's answer is no, it is always out of His great love for us and with His amazing grace.

David and I had been dating for about four months. I had this friend from work who was also dating a married guy. The four of us would go out together frequently. We had plans to go out one evening. That very afternoon, my friend came over to my apartment and said that they wouldn't be going with us and the reason was she had broken up with him. One thing is for sure. When God wants to get his point across to us, He has no lack of resources. Of course, whether we decide to listen or not is totally up to us. I have heard it said that God is a gentleman and will never *make* us do anything, but I am still so amazed at the lengths He will go to reach us. My friend announced to us that she had found Jesus and was born again. She had to break up with him because he was married. I felt as if a knife had been stuck in my heart. I knew the Lord was speaking right to me. Yet, once again, I decided not to listen.

You might think God would give up on me at this point. I thought He would. What's weird is I never stopped thinking about God. He was always in the back of my mind. In fact, I even asked for forgiveness if I was going to do something that I felt was really wrong or if I got scared. I had an extremely distorted view of God. I couldn't understand the love he had for me. I couldn't understand love in general.

David and I had been dating now for about six months. We had a great time. We would be out to all hours of the night drinking and partying. He took me to St. Thomas. He bought me jewelry, clothes, and TVs. *How could this relationship be bad?* I met his children. I liked them and they liked me. We even had a good time when we were with them. I drove by his home when I wasn't with him and saw him outside playing with his kids and I thought he was a wonderful father and he would be a wonderful father to our kids. What I didn't realize at the time is that things aren't always what they seem to be. It was as if we were on a prolonged vacation, but eventually reality was going to set in.

What I didn't know was that David's early years were a mess. He had a very hard life growing up. David's family looked normal to an outsider. He had a mother, father, and two sisters. However, his oldest sister was his half-sister. David and his other sister were the product of an affair his mother had and not blood related to the man they called "dad." David's biological father had his own family and wouldn't accept him as his son. He was treated cruelly and with great resentment from both men. His mother's husband knew David and his sister weren't his and had a hard time handling it. Although his biological father wouldn't acknowledge them as his, for fear of hurting his wife and current family, everyone knew the truth. But no one talked about it.

David was emotionally abused by his mother's husband and abandoned by his actual father. The emotional damage had been done and lived at the root of David's insecurity and abusive nature. His mother pleaded for his biological father to spend time with him. Reluctantly, he would sometimes take him and his other son "hunting." Hunting to them usually started before sunrise and ended up in the bars around noon. That is probably where David's issues with alcohol started.

Although David somehow developed an excellent work ethic, determined to make something of himself, he also established a strong drinking habit. He quit high school in the ninth grade and went to work, helping to support his mother and sisters. He had his own welding business at a very early age and he threw himself into the idea that he was going to be a huge success and make a lot of money. He got his current girlfriend pregnant at eighteen and had a son. They got married and moved in with his mother. A year and a half later he had a daughter.

Their marriage was a disaster. By the time he and I met, his children were nine and ten and their relationship was non-existent. We were two very broken people trying desperately to put our lives back together.

Then it happened. David and his wife filed for divorce. He asked me to quit my job and live with him and I did. We had an apartment in North Jersey. She kept the large house with the pool and Mercedes, a few towns away. He said the only thing he wanted was a couple of antique items that he had acquired over the years and his kids. He told me she was not a good mother and, from what I could see, that was true. The divorce started to get ugly and the fighting between them began. It was around the holidays and we were going to just have dinner at home. I made dinner and waited. Hours went by and he didn't come in. I tried to call him on his car phone, but he didn't answer. I finally went to bed. When he did come home, he told me that he had a meeting and couldn't get out of it. I found out a few weeks later that he had met his soon to be ex-wife for dinner. When I confronted him, he then explained that he had to talk about the kids and how they were going to handle the holidays. In his mind, it was a sensible thing to do. In mine, it was just another act of betrayal and something all too familiar to me. Our relationship changed from that time on. Distrust replaced trust and we fought often. I knew this was not the best relationship, but once again I thought I had no other choice. I was in survival mode. I decided to try to make this work.

All I wanted deep inside was to feel loved. I had no sense of self-worth. I developed the mentality that I had to please people in order to be loved and accepted. I took this into every area of my life. My home had to be spotless. If I cooked or baked, it had to be perfect. If I took a course at school, I had to get A's. I had to look perfect.

I was trying to be the mother David's children's own mother should've been. I baked for their school parties, I ironed all their clothes, I cooked everything from scratch, and I did their homework with them. We moved around a lot. David never paid the rent on time so many times we didn't get our lease renewed. Money was a problem. He had to pay his ex-wife alimony. His drinking was interfering with the way he handled his business. He was out all the time getting "business" he said, when in reality he was hanging out drinking. My mother-in-law moved in with us until the divorce was final.

David finally got custody of his kids. His ex-wife agreed to this as long as she got the house, car, and furnishings. After everything was finalized, she dropped off the kids' belongings on our porch and they didn't see her again until they went looking for her years later. At this time, we were renting a house up in northwestern New Jersey, on top of a mountain. It was around the area where David used to go hunting. It was a beautiful area, very isolated, with deer walking through our yard. We only had one car and David took it to work. Being out in the country, I had no way to go anywhere. There wasn't anything close to us that I could even walk to. I always had to wait for David to come home. We were trying to be a family, but it was like trying to put together a puzzle with the wrong pieces. I started to talk to him about God. He seemed interested and actually read the Bible. We took the kids to church once in a while. The problem was we all had our own baggage. I had my own mess and the kids had theirs. *What mother drops of her young kids and doesn't see them again?* She didn't pay much attention to them when they lived with her either. David never stopped drinking and partying, even when I was home with his kids. In fact his drinking was becoming more and more of a problem. I was trying to raise two children who I wasn't much older than and who I knew little about. When David did come home, he wasn't in any condition to help and just went to sleep. To make matters worse, he undermined what little authority I had with the children.

By the time the divorce was finalized, I was five months pregnant. My parents rushed around to put together a small wedding. We were married in November of 1977. My daughter was born in March of 1978. And oh how I fell in love with this little person! How thankful I was that she was perfect! I knew in my heart I didn't deserve it. *No way. Not after everything I had already done.* I vowed to give this child the best home I could. She would have all the love a person could want. I would always be there for her. I wanted everything perfect. The only problem was, nothing is ever perfect. David's older daughter became very jealous of her. David wasn't home at all and here I was trying to raise three kids. His drinking became more and more intolerable. The tension and fighting escalated. I started to resent his other children and our relationships crumbled. I lost it one night with his daughter. She was upset and telling me she was going to make her father leave the baby and me. I slapped her and said things I shouldn't have. Depressed and angry, I didn't know where to turn. I tried to talk to my mother about it, but her main concern was that I would come back home. She told me if it was that bad then I would have to go to a shelter. Not knowing where else to turn, I started praying for God to please intervene. *Please take the other children away.* I couldn't handle them and I didn't want to cause them any more pain either. Finally David took his other two children to live with his sister. He left me completely alone for two days, never telling me where he was or what he was doing, or if he was coming back. I was terrified and, once again, felt abandoned. David came back, but the relationship was more strained than ever.

Once again we had to move. This time we relocated to a small two-bedroom condo next to the town I grew up in. I was alone more now than ever. David came in late after our daughter was asleep and left early before she was up. There were nights David told me he was coming home and said he would take us out to eat. I would dress her up and we would wait and wait. Many times he just never showed up. When he did, he would be so intoxicated and I would be so angry, the fighting would start.

One night, slightly after midnight I got a call from the police. My husband had been shot and was in a hospital in Newark. His condition wasn't good and I was told to get up there as soon as I could. I left my daughter with my mother and my father drove me up to the hospital. There was an armed officer outside his room and as I approached they started questioning me. "Do you know what is going on?" No, I had no idea. No idea why he was shot. No idea why the police officer was outside his room. My head was spinning and I had a hard time believing what was happening.

I went into his room and he was hooked up to a number of machines. He had been shot behind his left ear and the bullet was lodged in his neck at the base of his spine. The doctors said that miraculously the bullet missed several major arteries or he would have died. He was struggling to speak as I leaned over him to hear what he was trying to tell me. He whispered, "It's not over. They're going to try and finish it." I start to shake. *What has he done?* I know him. He's cocky and arrogant and fears nothing, but doesn't he realize he has a baby daughter and wife at home, never mind two other children. As the details unfold I become so angry with him. *How could he put us in this spot?* My life felt like it was in a downward spiral. The more I tried to fix it, the worse it got. Seems in my husband's quest to make a lot of money, he stepped into a territory of business he shouldn't have. He didn't have any respect, as it was, for rules. He felt they weren't made for him. Somewhere, somehow in the course of his life he was led to believe that he was above the law. This instance wasn't a legal issue, but it was an issue nonetheless. There were people who controlled certain areas of a particular business and it was known to outsiders not to interfere. David saw an opportunity to make good money and didn't care that he wasn't welcome and insisted on pushing his way in. This time he ran up against someone who wasn't going to put up with it.

They can't operate to take out the bullet because of its location. It is too close to his spine. So they leave it in. The left side of David's face is paralyzed. They said they don't know if the paralysis will go away, only time will tell. In the meantime, David tells me that we have to leave the state for a while until things calm down. I don't even ask what he means. I didn't want to know. We leave and go to Florida for about two weeks. Finally he gets a call and we can go back home. The problem had been resolved for the time being.

With the other two children away at their aunt's house and business picking up somewhat, David borrowed money from a business partner and we moved to a much larger house in Lincroft. Funny, all the things that I thought would make my life easier - someone to take care of me and provide what I needed - didn't make anything better. I didn't like the relationship anymore. It was so strained. However, now I had a daughter whom I had vowed to give the best life I could to, and that made all the difference in what I decided to do. He would come home drunk and fall down on the front lawn and sleep there. I was embarrassed and feeling so alone again. I didn't like the person he had become, or maybe always was and I just hadn't noticed it. In my distorted way of thinking, I thought if I could only have another child it would make things better. He would have to be home more.

I finally became pregnant. I was happy and convinced that this pregnancy would change my marriage and family life for the better. I felt that I now had a chance to "be a family." In my quest to make everything better, I never stopped to consider that all I was doing was covering up the problems that were already there. You cannot change another person and you certainly can't fix emotional issues by adding on more emotional situations.

About three months into my pregnancy, I began to bleed. I went to the doctors and he told me it can sometimes happen and then stop, or I could be having a miscarriage. I didn't want to hear anything about a miscarriage, so I was determined to do what it took to keep the pregnancy. I was extremely careful. About a week later we went on vacation. We both loved the beach and we rented a small place down at the shore. I thought that a vacation would help me to relax and would be good for all of us. Halfway through the week, my bleeding increased. Still thinking I was having a miscarriage, I continued to try to do everything in my power to be careful and hopefully hold on to the pregnancy. The day we returned home from vacation, not only was the bleeding getting heavier but I now had pain. Later in the afternoon the pain became so severe that I had to crawl into the bathroom. Reluctantly I conceded to going to the emergency room. I had my parents come and pick up my daughter.

During the examination, the doctor told me that he didn't like what he didn't see. I was scheduled for more tests. The results showed that I was definitely pregnant, only the pregnancy wasn't in my uterus. It was in my fallopian tube. I had an ectopic pregnancy and I needed emergency surgery. During the surgery, my right fallopian tube had to be removed. They told me after the surgery that I was a very lucky girl. I had hemorrhaged a pint of blood into my abdomen. If I hadn't gone to the hospital when I did, I would not have made it.

After a week in the hospital I finally was able to go home. I was depressed and discouraged, wondering why things always had to be so hard for me. My grandmother came over to visit me one afternoon. I loved my grandmother. She was a shy, quiet woman, with a contagious laugh. She also had her share of hard times, but what I remember the most about her was how strong a person she was. Not physically, but emotionally. Whenever we met her at restaurant for dinner, we would be able to find exactly where she was by her laughter that rang out over all the other noise in the place. This particular afternoon we sat on the couch talking. I told her that I had had enough. I wasn't going to try and have another child. I just couldn't handle any more heartache. She looked at me and in a tone I never heard her use before she said, "You don't ever give up. You're much stronger than that." Many times in the years following, when difficult times came, I would hear her saying those words to me.

It took a good month for me to get back on my feet. After trying to become pregnant again without success and after a lot of testing, I found out that my remaining tube was completely blocked. I could not have another child without intervention.

Chapter 9

"The LORD himself goes before you and will be with you; He will never leave you nor forsake you. "Do not be afraid; do not be discouraged" (Deuteronomy 31:8).

David began making amazing progress. He still had the feeding tube in place because his throat had suffered damage from the long period of time he was intubated. He needed to be tested to see if they could start him on soft foods. The fear was if his throat wasn't working properly, food and/or water could end up in his lungs causing severe problems. Once again, they couldn't say if he would ever be able to have his feeding tube removed to eat normally.

It was explained to me that during those twelve minutes without oxygen, David's body was beginning to shut down. There are electrical pathways in our brains that help us function the way we do and those had started to breakdown. He would have to relearn how to walk, speak, eat, etc. The normal functions we take for granted were completely lacking. Yet, I knew if he could never eat again and would have to remain on the feeding tube, he wouldn't want to live. David failed the first swallow test they gave him and my heart sank. He had come a long way, but he still had so far to go. The question was, would he continue to make enough progress so insurance would continue to pay and keep him there?

David, at this time, was still not able to comprehend a lot of what we were discussing. Although he now knew what year it was and who was president, he had absolutely no recollection of what had happened to him over the last two and a half months. As I continued to pray for David and watch him recover, I noticed that it was beginning to become easier to forgive him for causing us so much pain. Seeing how vulnerable he was, made me realize that no one starts out his or her day saying, "I'm going to become an alcoholic." There are life situations and choices we make in handling those situations that send us down those roads. I don't think I would be here today, with the choices I have made, without God's hand upon me. I definitely know that I would not be the person I am, or be where I am, without Him.

We were playing a waiting game, hoping and praying that David would continue to improve. There were days when David wouldn't cooperate with the physical therapy instructors. We tried to tell him if he didn't cooperate he couldn't stay where he was and that I couldn't afford to take him home. Home health care was almost as expensive as the nursing home facility. His children and grandchildren, as well as close friends came to visit. We took him out on Father's Day to go to his grandson's baseball game. He was wheelchair-bound and could now sit up straight in a chair, but was not able to walk even with the help of a walker. What concerned me the most was that as well as he was doing, it was very obvious that he didn't realize the damage that had been done to him, how much further he had to go, and the possibility that he may never recover completely.

The news of what had happened and how God had miraculously intervened and was healing David spread quickly. I, along with others close to David, were still praying for complete healing and for him to be able to come home. I had a pretty good idea how much more he needed to regain before I could bring him home and people at the rehab were still not able to tell me if that was a possibility. I also knew that he would have to be pretty self-sufficient because I still had to work and could not afford full time in home care. Although I have seen God heal in an instant, I also know that sometimes it is a process. I couldn't help but think that if God had delivered and healed David instantaneously and he didn't have to go through all of the rehabilitation processes, maybe then he would have been easily swayed back into drinking and the lifestyle he had lived.

David continued to make the progress needed to continue his stay in rehab. He began to learn to use the phone and the television remote. I knew he needed to get well enough to come home, but I also liked the fact that my home was so peaceful. I was in control of the money and bills were paid on time. I paid off the credit cards he had run up and I even had money left over after the bills were paid. I began to realize that David had been spending over $400 a week in alcohol and other expenses that I wasn't aware of. I had not had that kind of peace in my home in over thirty years and I didn't want that to change. I also wondered how he would handle not drinking if he got well enough to come home and be on his own. *What if he started drinking again?* I knew I could not go through any more, but I started to feel guilty about the way I felt.

All through this whole ordeal, from the time David coded in the hospital, not one member of my family, outside of my children, came to sit with me or to see how David was doing. Not one of them offered any support. Even if they didn't like David or agree with the way he was, didn't they think my children and I could use the company? This lack of affection, this conditional love, has served as my biggest obstacle when it comes to understanding how real love operates. Learning that God loves me unconditionally and that He isn't standing there waiting for me to mess up has always been a challenge for me. This performance-based mentality is so ingrained in my mind that I have to daily meditate on God's Word and seek revelation from him as to how he sees me and his will for me.

I tried to reach out to my mother when my children were growing up and had sports games or events at school. Sometimes she would come, but many times her response was, "They have you there. They don't need me." No, maybe they didn't need her there, but they wanted her there. I wanted her there. I needed her support. Thankfully, I do have some wonderful friends that were there for us through this whole ordeal. Without them, it would have been an even more difficult road, that's for sure. I was not *expecting* the support from my family, but I was *hoping* it might be different. I came to realize that my true family is the family of God. We belong to an amazing family and nothing will ever change that. We are sealed with a promise from God that, although people may hurt and disappoint us, He will never leave us nor forsake us.

Chapter 10

"Praise the LORD, my soul, and forget not all his benefits—who forgives all your sins and heals all your diseases, who redeems your life from the pit and crowns you with love and compassion" **(Psalm 103:2-4).**

When we accept Jesus as Lord of our life a really truly supernatural thing happens. We are reborn, and become a new creation, one that has never existed before. We don't necessarily see the change all at once, but we are His and nothing short of us saying we don't want Him anymore will ever make Him leave us. The Bible says if we seek Him with all of our heart, we will find Him. I believe that is why people know Him on different levels. It is the amount of time and energy we are willing to put into finding Him and how much we really want Him that makes the difference. I was beginning to realize that nothing I chased after in this life was bringing me satisfaction or peace for that matter. I was just adding layer upon layer to my own misery. Maybe because I struggled so hard from such an early age that I had a very strong will of my own to survive. The problem is our will so often gets in the way of God's will for our lives. My whole life I always heard people blame bad things on God. Natural disasters occur and it's "an act of God" or someone gets a horrible disease and "it must be God's will." I always had a real problem trying to pray for God's will in my life. I was afraid of what His will for me might be. I had so much to learn about God and what His will for us actually meant. I needed to understand what His love was really like. He knew all of this and, when I look back, I realize just how patient and loving a Father he really is. God's timing is perfect and He's never late. Just when we think we may have run too far away from God for Him to even think about us anymore, He shows up and it's always at the perfect time.

We lived in a big house in a very affluent part of Lincroft. It was everything David had been striving for - the big home, the nice cars, the clothes, expensive restaurants, and travel. David was making good money, but he still did not know how to handle it. He bought what he wanted first and then paid what had to be paid afterward. The problem was with his kind of business, the money didn't always come in when it should. A job could be finished and the company could take up to three months to pay. If he didn't put aside and prepare for this, and David didn't, he could end up owing a lot of people money. David handled all the money. That's how he wanted it. He gave me what I needed for food shopping and clothes and such, but I had no idea what our financial position was. What I didn't realize at the time was that David owed a lot of money to the IRS. Oblivious to what was going on with our finances, my focus was on making our marriage and home stronger. I wanted to have another child.

Right around this time, I met a woman down the street with a child my daughter's age and we became friendly. We found out that we had a lot in common and our girls became very close friends. Lynda was a born again Christian and went to a church a few towns over. She was very open about her faith and beliefs and, for the first time in a long time, I started to talk about my faith and my life. I began to open up to her. She invited me to go to her church and from then on my life truly began to change.

I started pursing doctors about the possibility of having another child. I had tests done and was told that my remaining fallopian tube was completely blocked and if I truly wanted another child I would have to see a specialist. They sent me to the University of Pennsylvania. I confided in Lynda about what was going on. A week or so before my first appointment at the specialist, Lynda called me and told me that God could heal me. "All you have to do is believe that He will." She said she was going to church that day and that she would go up for prayer for me. *I didn't even have to be there? I just had to believe that God would do this for me?* I had been going to church, praying, and reading my Bible. It was all very new to me, but I started to believe that maybe God hadn't totally left me and maybe He did love me and would heal me. I didn't think about what I had done or been through. I just decided to believe. Later that afternoon, David and I went to the food store and I waited in the car while he went inside. Sitting there, all-of-a-sudden, I had this sharp, warm sensation in my left side, the side where my tube was blocked. It subsided as quickly as it began. At this time David had been attending church with me once in a while and I was openly talking to him about God. To my amazement, he seemed interested. When he got back in the car, I told him what Lynda had told me about God being able to heal me and about the pain in my side and that I believed that God had just opened up my tube. Surprisingly, he didn't tell me I was crazy or stupid for believing that. He said he was glad and we would see when we went to the doctor.

A week later we went to Pennsylvania to see the specialist. Once in the doctor's office, we went over my records and history. He discussed a couple of options with me. He told me that I could have reconstructive surgery of my tube, but the success rate of that surgery was slim and I could very easily end up with another ectopic pregnancy. He also suggested a new procedure at that time, In-vitro fertilization. Unfortunately, the success rate of that procedure at that time was also very small. He suggested that because I had one healthy child, to concentrate on that, and forget about trying for another. I was almost in tears. To my surprise, my husband spoke up and told the doctor that we had been going to church and believed that my tube was clear. He asked if he would please repeat the test that had already been done. The doctor said that was a waste of time and he could do another more invasive procedure to go in and look around. David was persistent and finally the doctor agreed to repeat the test that I had done a few months before. I think by that time he just wanted to get us out of his office.

The day we left for the test I was nervous and called my mother before I left to let her know what we were doing and that I believed that I was healed and would have a good report. I wanted some support from her. I never gave up trying to get some type of encouragement from her. I could hear the tone in her voice as she told me not to get my hopes up. I would so often hang up from talking to my mother and just cry. She never seemed to be happy for me. I never heard, "You're doing a great job" or "I'm proud of you." I wanted so desperately to hear that from her. This time though, I was determined not to let it get me down. I still believed that I would be able to have another child.

We arrived at the doctor's office around 10 am. It seemed to take forever to get them to take me in. This faith stuff was all still so new to me. To think that God wanted good things for me was hard for me to grasp, but I gave it everything I had. I started to wonder if I was a little crazy believing in all of it. The church that I attended was an Assembly of God church. They taught from the Bible and had prayer for healing, but I never really saw much healing going on in the church. I knew I didn't deserve any special treatment from God, especially after all I had done, but I figured maybe, just maybe, I didn't know this God very well after all. It took a while for the nurse to get me prepped and it was uncomfortable. When I get nervous I have a tendency to talk quickly, and about anything, just to have someone talk to me. The nurse with me never responded and didn't even crack a smile. I could see there wasn't going to be any encouragement from her, so I just laid back and prayed as hard as I could. Finally, the doctor came in and started the procedure. It seemed an eternity before he said anything. He asked me a couple of questions and then said, "I don't see any blockage in your tube. It is completely clear." I couldn't believe my ears. I wanted to be so happy, but I was afraid I hadn't heard him right. I got dressed and went out to my husband and daughter and told them what I thought he said. I could tell that David was surprised. Tia was so happy. As young as she was, she understood that this made her mom and dad really happy. When we got home, I actually made David call the office to double check that I had heard him right. Sure enough, everything was fine and we could try for another child. My whole family was amazed at the results. Even though they were skeptical of my faith and the church I attended, my father and mother started coming to services. My father became very involved and one Sunday on a day I will never forget, he made his way up to the altar to accept Jesus as his Savior.

Chapter 11

"Call to me and I will answer you and tell you great and unsearchable things you do not know" (Jeremiah 33:3).

In the beginning of his rehab days, he slipped back frequently into the coma emergence state and did all kinds of strange things. He saw people who weren't really there, called out directions to his men on a job he did twenty some years ago, and he also got so mad at me thinking that I had sold our home and bought the place that he was in. When we finally got through to him that it wasn't our home but a hospital, he would yell at our son, Jacob, to go get the car and get him out of there. Most of what he talked about was from years earlier. He had lost his memory of recent times and didn't understand the condition he was in.

Thankfully, he became more and more lucid and those times of confusion became less and less. He became physically stronger and, after about a month and a half, he was able to start using a walker. They got more aggressive with his physical therapy and he made amazing progress. I think everyone in the place was amazed at the transformation that was taking place. Everyone began calling him a miracle. By the end of two months, the office manager called me into her office and told me that while David had made such amazing progress she didn't think that insurance would continue to cover him after that week. David was still very weak and had a feeding tube. I applied for family medical leave and was granted 10 weeks. I was happy for that, but I knew that David needed more time in therapy there before I would be able to help him at home by myself. I also knew that 10 weeks would go by too quickly. I couldn't physically lift David and he couldn't lift himself up out of a chair or bed at this point yet. He couldn't walk up or down stairs. He needed to learn how to walk and use his hands again.

I had just seen God do such an amazing thing in our lives and although no one else could give me any answers, I had this amazing confidence that my God would work things out for us. I just had no idea how. I learned at this time to pray, believe, and step out. It was a confidence that went beyond my comprehension. It was a peace that passed all understanding. There was also a joy that kept bubbling up inside of me knowing that God, Almighty God, creator of all things, cared about my family and me. That he would pay attention to the smallest details of our lives was so amazing to me. It's one thing to hear about it and quite another to experience it.

It was coming down to the wire now. They were telling me to make other plans as to where we would take David. I told them I couldn't afford a place that insurance wouldn't pay for, so I would have to take him home and care for him myself. The manager said that it wasn't wise for me to do that. I insisted that there was no other way. She told me she would try to get a couple more weeks, but not to get my hopes up. She came back two days later and told me David could have two more weeks in the rehab, that insurance would cover it, and then said she had never seen that happen before. They began to instruct me on how to take care of David once he left their facility. They taught me how to feed David through the tube and keep it clean. Although it was relatively easy, I knew this is not how David would want to live. I prayed, "God, I know you didn't bring him this far to just let him go. Your word says you have good plans for us to give us a hope and a future." I gave David that scripture to hold onto. We scheduled another test to see if his swallowing had improved enough to take the tube out. This time David was able to sit up straight and participate better than the last time. The familiar old phrase that had come to haunt us every step of the way, "We just don't know how far he will progress" was used yet again. To everyone's amazement, David passed the test and was able to start introducing foods and liquids orally. It had been over four months without eating or drinking anything by mouth. Now he had to learn how to get control of his hands to feed himself.

We started making preparations to take David home. We had to get a commode and a shower seat to help out in the bathroom. We needed to have a gate made for the top of the stairs to prevent him from falling down them. David was very unstable at this point, even with a walker, and the doctors feared that if he did fall, he could have a stroke because of the blood thinner he was on. Extra care had to be taken so he wouldn't fall out of bed or off of the couch. He would have to have someone with him at all times and could not be left alone. Finally, the day came to take him home.

The next two months I spent all of my time taking care of David, helping him get around, to shower, and to eat. Some nights were very difficult. He would wake up yelling at someone or something and insist that there were people in the room. David slept on the living room couch at first. His bed was higher off the ground than the couch and we were afraid if he fell off, he would get seriously hurt. I came out one morning to find that all the cushions from the couch were on the dining room table under his favorite lamp. He explained that he thought it was going to fall so he was going to take it down. Another night when our oldest grandson slept over, he called Mark out to move the living room table out of the way because a train was coming through. Poor Mark was confused, but quickly moved the table. Then, at that moment David realized what he thought was happening wasn't real. This was an important turning point for him. It was the first time he was aware of the difference between reality and fantasy and I took it as a sign that he was going to come back enough for me to be able to keep him home. Although at this point, doctors still had no idea how much his brain would heal, God had let me see enough to keep on hoping and believing.

Time was running out and I would have to go back to work. David was still making slow progress, but not enough to be left alone for an hour or so. I couldn't afford private in-home help and insurance would only pay for someone to come in a certain amount of hours a week and only for a set amount of time. Between those people, my son who worked shift work as a police officer, and a close friend of the family we worked it out so that most of the time David had someone with him. One thing I have learned from all that I have been through is that God's timing is always perfect, never early and never late, but always on time. Many times it was not my timing but His and learning to trust and lean on that was not easy. I felt that I needed to know ahead of time what I would do. I needed to plan the future. That was one of the most difficult areas for me to give over to the Lord.

The last week that I was home, I remember thinking how much better David seemed to me. He wasn't going through as many of those episodes and his realization of what was real and what wasn't was getting stronger. It was as if a haze was beginning to lift and things were becoming so much clearer to him. He also began to ask questions about what had happened to him. Bits and pieces were beginning to come together, although he still had no recollection of going into the hospital. He remembered nothing of what happened there and for most of the next two months. The stronger he became and the more his mind healed, the more he wanted to start doing. He began to get frustrated. I had to remind him of how far he had come and the advice that was given to him at the rehab. "You are going to have to learn to laugh at yourself and take it one day at a time."

I don't know why I still get amazed, but I do. I don't believe we'll ever know enough about our God to stop getting amazed. Seeing the miracles taking place in front of me was overwhelming. David began to improve in leaps and bounds. I was only back to work about four weeks and David stopped needing someone with him. God had worked it out so I only had to put a small amount of money out of my own pocket since the day David went into the hospital. My bills were being paid and I had no need to worry over any of my finances. Little did I realize, at this point, that I still had not seen the most amazing miracle that God had done through this whole process.

Chapter 12

"Every good and perfect gift is from above, coming down from the Father of the heavenly lights, who does not change like shifting shadows" (James 1:17).

David's drinking was escalating. I was so frustrated trying to become pregnant. I was still under the impression that if I could just become pregnant with a second child we would have a real family and things would change. Business wasn't going that well and he spent more and more time trying to make it better. He was consumed with becoming a success and it didn't matter what else he had to sacrifice.

I finally became pregnant. I was ecstatic! Things seemed to be going very well until the third month. I started to bleed. I remember thinking, *This can't be.* Why would God heal me to have another child and then have something go wrong? The bleeding continued to worsen and finally the doctor told me that sometimes this happens. There could be something wrong with the fetus and that I would lose the baby. I went home and tried to get ahold of David. He was not answering calls, which only meant one thing - he was out drinking. I got the message to him through his secretary, but he still didn't get home until later that evening. He had been drinking heavily and we fought. He then fell asleep on the living room couch.

I felt so alone and abandoned, not only by my husband, but also by God. *Why did he let this happen?* I started getting severe cramps so I went into my bedroom, laid down on my bed, and cried. I had been trying so hard to do everything I could to make things better. I had even tried to become pregnant a certain time of year so that I would have the baby in the spring and would be able to lose the weight for summer. I was still trying to be in control, still wanting everything to be perfect. I said I was trusting in God, but I never completely let go. I was always trying to do things on my terms. I wanted to fill the void in my life. I was still trying to fix everything myself. I wanted this child so much, yet I wanted it on my terms.

I had been through so much - first, the ectopic and losing that pregnancy, then not being able to get pregnant, then getting healed, and now having a miscarriage while my husband is drunk, asleep, and indifferent to what is happening. Finally, I began to realize that I needed to let go. I was beginning to understand that trying to be perfect all the time wasn't what God wanted from me. He loved me and wanted good things for my life, but there were these layers of pain and abuse that had to be undone. I was praying and telling God I was sorry for trying to manipulate and control everything and that if He didn't want me to have another child then, although I still wanted one so badly, I would accept it. I felt a warm presence wrap itself around me and I fell asleep. When I woke up in the morning, I lost the baby and realized that I had slept through the worst part. I believe God held me during the night, let me sleep while the contractions were going on, and woke me when it was over. I had never felt such a warm, loving presence in my life as I did that night. That morning I had to go to the hospital and they performed a DNC. I was told that I had to wait three months, but I would be able to try again.

David was still drinking, but he was also attending church on and off. My prayer life was growing and so was my relationship with the Lord. I was determined that my daughter would be brought up to know the Lord also. I remembered how on fire I was for Jesus when I was first saved and that same desire to know Him more was rekindled in me.

One Sunday we went to church and I could sense the tension as soon as I walked in the door. For me, the church was a place of stability and peace. What we experienced this day was anything but that. The church board wanted to get rid of our pastor. The church was divided. Half of the congregation was on the side of the church board and the other half was siding with the pastor. The pastor stood up at the front of the church and announced that all those who wanted to stay with him should come up and stand with him. I didn't understand what he had done. I felt comfortable with this man. I was new in my faith and this man was a very dynamic speaker who appeared to have the answers to so many things I was seeking. I was putting this man in a place in my heart that was only meant for God and I was looking to him for answers. I went up with the people that wanted to stay with him. I left the church that day with all of those who had sided with the pastor. I was shaking and confused. I would later on realize that God is the one and only one to hold that place in our hearts.

In the meantime, we needed a place to worship and fellowship. David and I had a large home with a huge cellar so I went to David and asked if I could offer our home for the time being. To my surprise, he said yes. I was thrilled! We held Sunday morning and evening services as well as Wednesday night services in my basement. I thought for sure that David would become a strong believer now. *He was tithing and offering his home for the church, surely he would stop drinking and be the husband and father he was meant to be.* We held services in our home for six months. More and more people began to attend. We were outgrowing my cellar so they began to look for a larger place to meet. To my dismay and confusion, David also started to miss services. He still allowed me to tithe, but what I didn't realize was that, for David, this was a show of what he had. His heart wasn't in the right place. His drinking began to escalate again. One night David came home so drunk he fell on the front lawn and couldn't get up. Our neighbor and pastor came over and carried him inside.

One of the most beautiful things about letting go and putting it in God's hands is that we then get to see what His desires are. There is a scripture in the Bible, Psalm 37:4, that reads, "Take delight in the Lord and he will give you the desires of your heart." A few months later I finally did become pregnant and the beauty of it was it was exactly at the time of year that I had desired to be pregnant, but this time it wasn't my doing, it was His. It's the little details like this that I find show me how much our Heavenly Father loves us and how intimately He knows us. Nine months later, I gave birth to my son Jacob and what a beautiful miracle he has been to me!

At the same time all of this was going on, the IRS caught up with David. He hadn't been paying his taxes for his business. They put a levy on all of David's business accounts and for six months we had no income. My house was now in foreclosure, my car was repossessed, and bill collectors were calling non-stop. We were holding church services in my basement, so I thought for sure God would let me keep the house. We can get caught up in so many things if we are not careful. We can follow people for the wrong reason. The church I was in was a very legalistic church. It was a works based church. "If you do this for God, then he will do this for you." God sees the whole picture when we only see glimpses here and there. That's why it is so important to lean not on our own understanding, but in all our ways acknowledge God and He will direct our paths.

There was so much that was going on with David that I didn't know about the way we came to get our house, the money he owed, the taxes we hadn't paid, and the way he threw his money around. I was in my own little world, but now my world was being shaken again. What seemed like the end of so much for me would really only be a new beginning into a new journey of God's amazing grace.

Chapter 13

"My soul thirsts for God, for the living God" (Psalm 42:2).

We had to sell our house in Lincroft to avoid foreclosure. At the last minute, a lawyer friend of mine from church said he had a buyer for us. We sold the house and walked away with only twenty thousand dollars because we had to sell the house far below its value. David was so angry with me. He had wanted us to go bankrupt, but I didn't want to. He blamed me for losing the house. We found a small house to rent in the town next to where I grew up. The day we moved in, David dropped me off with my daughter and three month old son and left. I was devastated. People from the church came over and helped me clean it up and move in. Once again, I was abandoned. I was so hurt. It wasn't my fault the way things had turned out and yet he blamed me.

I had grown enough in my walk with my Lord to know that I was not completely alone. Part of me wanted to put up the defenses and do whatever it took to survive. The other part of me knew that it was time to pray, forgive, and let God do what he does best, restore. Every time I got to the place where I had enough and wanted to leave David for good, I would pray and tell God. Then someway, somehow, David would always come around, promise to try harder, and I would forgive him.

Over the next fourteen years we lived like that. I focused on my children. I went to church and raised my children in the Lord. During this time David stayed away from church. He drank a lot. We didn't have the money we needed to pay the bills on time. Our utilities were always being shut off. Our house went into and out of foreclosure. Everywhere I went, I went with friends or family because David was always too busy working or out. There was a time when Jacob hadn't seen his father for two weeks before he finally asked where he was. I kept praying and believing, but I wasn't seeing any results. I was getting to the point where I just wanted my husband out and to get on with my own life. My problem was I didn't have any money at all to fall back on. I couldn't even divorce him and get half of everything. There wasn't anything to get half of. We didn't have health insurance, never mind life insurance.

The cops were at our house periodically either to arrest David for not paying alimony to his first wife or because he hadn't shown up for some court appearance where he was required. I didn't even tell people half of what went on for fear that they wouldn't believe I was telling the truth. I was trying to live this life that appeared normal when there was absolutely nothing normal about my existence. I carried around this shame and guilt all the time, afraid that people would see what was really going on and that I wouldn't be accepted anywhere. I was finally at the point where I didn't care about making everything work anymore. I was resigned to the fact that I could not do it. I had tried everything I knew how.

I had been praying for a job. Jacob was thirteen at this time and I really didn't want to leave him alone after school but I was tired of never having any money and, although I hadn't wanted to, I felt I needed to work. I got a job at the university near my house. The pay wasn't great, but I had health insurance and some steady income.

One weekend, when Jacob was fifteen years old, I went to a prayer meeting at a friend's house down the road. It was a different kind of prayer meeting. We sang and prayed and just practiced being in the presence of God. For the first time I really began to experience the presence of God. It was a different level of closeness to Him. I went from thinking of Him as only God and Lord to Abba, Father. A new dimension of His love opened up to me. I was beginning to be able to allow this amazing love of God to heal the shattered pieces of my heart. A new world of worshipping an amazing God opened up to me and I became very hungry for more. This love that He was showing me was the very thing I needed to fill this hollow, empty void inside of me. I began to experience God on a different level. I started to believe that my God, the Creator of the universe, loved me with a love I had never before experienced. It was unconditional and it gave me a new found hope.

The following Monday morning, David came into my bedroom and sat on the edge of my bed and told me he didn't feel well. He was soaked with sweat and shaking. He said he fell in the bathroom and hit his head. There was blood everywhere. I told him to go lie down and I would take him to the emergency room. He said, "No rush. You can shower first." So I did, completely unaware of how serious the situation was. I finally got ready and took him to the emergency room. As soon as they examined David, they began rushing around prepping him and moving very quickly. They explained that he was having a massive heart attack. Once again faced with an emergency situation, I went into safety mode. I guess the doctors could tell that I was a little out of it. They came up to me asking me if I realized what was going on. I said I did, but in reality nothing was sinking in. They rushed him to another hospital where he would need to have triple bypass surgery. For the next few hours all I did was answer questions. After sifting through all the information, they realized how heavy a drinker David was and said before they could operate on him they needed to detox him. They put a pump in him to keep his heart going and sedated him very heavily. He then came down with pneumonia. Finally after three weeks, he was well enough so they could operate. They performed what they said at the time was a "successful triple by-pass" and for the next few months David sat home recovering. He had gone through detox and wasn't drinking.

Instead of him getting progressively better as they said he would, his condition deteriorated. It had been six months and he was becoming weaker and his breathing was becoming more labored once again. Concerned about what was happening and not getting any clear answers from the doctors here, we decided to take him to a specialist in New York, at NYU. Upon the initial examination, they explained that the first surgery was done incorrectly and David would need to have another triple bypass. This time, he would need to have his heart valve repaired and it needed to be done immediately. This would mean another three to six months of recovery during which time David would not be working. All we would have was what I was making and it would not be enough for us to survive.

This time David's surgery was a success. Although it is an amazing teaching hospital with highly skilled doctors, the hospital itself was dirty and the facilities were uncomfortable. After his surgery, David was placed in a large open recovery room with numerous patients and no privacy at all. David asked to be moved, but no room was available and it didn't look like there was going to be anything anytime soon. Hating hospitals and being the stubborn person he is, he insisted on leaving the hospital before the doctors would discharge him. He signed himself out. Against their insistence that David stay, four days after surgery I brought him home on the ferry from New York. Hardly able to walk, I helped David down the gangway and into the car. As we headed home, I was concerned about how much care he would need and how I would handle it. I had to work and was unable to stay home with David. Insurance paid for a nurse to come in three days a week and check on him. Our son Jacob was home after school to help if needed. Most of the time David spent on the couch recovering.

Chapter 14

"Can a mother forget the baby at her breast and have no compassion on the child she has borne? Though she may forget, I will not forget you!" (Isaiah 49:15).

My mother hardly ever did anything without my father. I don't remember her having any outside interests or friends that she would go out with. She would always be right at my father's side. So, when he started attending church she would be there with him. My father talked about the Lord to me. He also witnessed to people about Jesus. It was so amazing to me to see the transformation he had gone through. I did not notice much of a change in my mother. I do know, however, that she was listening in church because one day she called me up and said she needed to apologize for something. She said that in service they were talking about asking for forgiveness for anything you have done to hurt someone. The teaching was if you don't confess your sins, then God won't forgive you. She proceeded to tell me that when I was younger and going through those tough times, she wished I would die. I knew she was asking for my forgiveness, so I told her I forgave her, but when I hung up the phone I broke down and sobbed. I couldn't understand, being a mother myself, how any mother could wish her child dead. As hard as it was to hear those words, it made me realize that there was a legitimate reason why I felt such a lack of love and why I struggled so hard to be loved.

My father passed away a few years after all this happened. My mother emotionally fell apart. She couldn't function. She was angry and bitter at God for allowing this to happen to my father and to her. She told me she would always pray that God wouldn't take this man from her. My father had been her whole world. I was not that close with my mother, but something inside of me hurt so bad for her. I hated to drop her off alone at her house and see her watch until we were out of sight. I spent any spare time I had with her. I came home from work and she would come over for dinner. I took her shopping and went with her where she had to go, just so she wouldn't feel so alone. I don't know why, but I worried so much about her. Maybe I felt that now that she needed me, she would love me and approve of what I was doing.

With David being out of work for so long and waiting for Social Security Disability to kick in, our bills were adding up quickly. We were in a very bad situation financially. The money coming in wasn't enough to pay the bills and our mortgage was over six months behind. We had received notices of foreclosure. One day, my mother, knowing how bad things were suggested that we come live with her. She said she needed someone with her and we needed a place to go. I was not convinced in my heart this was a good thing to do, but I felt I had no other option, so I jumped at the invitation.

We went to her house and started to prepare to move in. We painted and fixed up a room for Jacob. David and I had to take the middle room and use the kid's old bunk beds. It wasn't convenient but it was a place to stay. Immediately, I began to sense that something was very wrong. I knew my mother was obsessive about cleaning and her routine. I knew that from growing up with her, from the times she would come in and tear the sheets out from under me because it was time for her to do the wash even if I didn't have to get up. I was never allowed to go into the refrigerator without her calling out from some room in the house, "What are you looking for?" Because I knew this, I tried to prevent any problems by cleaning up after us constantly. I realized very quickly that it didn't matter what I did. It just wasn't going to work.

My mother didn't like David and she let it show. David tried very hard to make it work. He had recovered well from the second surgery and he started to repair things around the house and fix it up. My mother had a septic tank and she was afraid it wouldn't be able to handle as many people as she now had living there, so David put in a sewer line for her and saved her thousands of dollars by doing it himself. He fenced in her yard. We did her lawn work. She didn't have a mortgage, so we paid her taxes, her utilities and purchased food for allowing us to stay there. One of her complaints was that she always had to eat alone, so we made sure we had dinners together. Nothing I could do was good enough. It was becoming unbearable. She kept saying that it wasn't going to work, us being there.

She would stand behind me when I did the dishes and tell me to put the dish detergent down under the counter. "Don't leave it up on the sink." I wasn't done using it, but she insisted that it didn't stay there. She called me from work one day and yelled at me for putting two pots away together. They didn't belong together and now they were stuck. Jacob wasn't allowed to watch TV in the family room. He had to stay in his room. He wasn't allowed to use her phone either. I had my washer and dryer downstairs in the basement, but for something quick I would use hers instead of running all the way downstairs. I was informed that I couldn't use her washer and dryer anymore. She was very upset one day, yelling at how we had put the trash in the garbage can outside the wrong way.

David was so upset, he starting drinking again. He went out and then came home and went to bed in the middle of the afternoon to avoid her. This infuriated her even more. We couldn't stand being home. Jacob was spending most of his time with his friends and we went over to my daughter's for dinner as often as we could. We couldn't stand being there. It all came to a head one night. I came home from having dinner at Tia's and she was ranting about how this wasn't a hotel. She was slamming doors. I finally went in to talk to her and she just sat there with this cold stare as I was talking. In desperation I said to her, "We never could talk." She just looked at me and said, "I know." She then told me we had to get out and if we didn't, she would get us out. I told her we didn't have anywhere to go and we didn't have the money to move anywhere. She said she didn't care. That she was beyond caring for me.

Although I always felt the lack of warmth and feeling from her, the reality of hearing it from her cut me deep. I was being kicked out with nowhere to go by the one person in the world who was supposed to care what happened to me. She wanted us out so badly that she said she would give me the security for whatever place I found. I finally found a small condo to rent a town over. I didn't want to take anything from her, so I went to my church to ask for help. They would give us enough for one month, but not the security. So I ended up going to my mother for the rest of the money I needed. When I approached her with this, she looked at me again and said, "I'll have to ask my *children* if I can give it to you." She said it with such coldness, it took me back for a minute. *Hadn't she said she would give it to me? Wasn't I one of her "children?"* It was as if she had stuck a knife in my chest. The pain felt so real. I couldn't get out of there fast enough.

Although this was one of the most painful times in my life and, at first I couldn't understand how a God who loved me would allow it to happen, I slowly began to realize a few things. I believe he allowed it to show me where a lot of my pain came from so that I could begin to heal. He opened my eyes and made me realize that so much of the hurt I had experienced as a child wasn't something I had imagined or misunderstood, and that it certainly wasn't my fault. It was part of a healing process that was just beginning to take place.

David had a small settlement from a job come in and we had a little money for a while. I also had to pull out the little bit of retirement money I had started to save from my job to help us afford to stay where we were. David was attempting to collect worker's comp because his heart attack was job related. I had nothing to do with my mother. I didn't call her. I didn't go see her. It was a few months before I even spoke to her and then it was only out of necessity. As I began to try to pull together the pieces of my life once again, David drank more and more heavily. The case for worker's compensation was not going well and we were running out of the money we had. I had left a new washer, dryer, refrigerator, and freezer at my mother's because there was no place to store it where we were. She informed me that I had to get it out of her basement. I had hoped to be able to store it there until we were able to find a place where I could use it. She insisted it had to come out, so I had to sell it.

David didn't have the hope that I had and he certainly wasn't trusting God to help us, so his only consolation was in his drinking. His heart was damaged because of the heart attack and surgeries and the heavy drinking was slowly destroying it even more. I came home one night to the house filled with smoke from a pot left burning on the stove. The smoke was so thick that I couldn't see David asleep on the couch across the room. That's when I decided it was time to leave. My son was now 18 and in college. I told him I was leaving, if for no other reason than to maybe wake David up. Both of my children told me a number of times that they understood if I couldn't take it anymore and wanted to leave. I just didn't want to tear my son's life apart more than it had already been. I wanted to see him through college and land a job. I wanted to see him get out on his own if I could wait that long, but I couldn't. I called my daughter and she said I could come stay with her. I was there two days and I got a call from Jacob. He had found his father in the living room and he had taken a whole bottle of pills along with the alcohol. He was rushed to the hospital where they revived him.

Jacob begged me not to leave again. He was so concerned what his father would do. As much as David had put us through being an abusive husband and father, our children still loved him and cared for him. Jacob was going for a degree in criminal justice and, at the same time all of this was going on, he was learning about this type of behavior in school. It gave him a better insight as to what was wrong with his father and actually gave him more compassion instead of anger for him. Tia loved her father, but the hurt that she suffered from him was, at times, too difficult for her to deal with. She was much angrier than her brother. I moved back home, still praying and believing for God to intervene somehow, but I was becoming very disillusioned. I started praying, "God who would want my kind of faith if they have to live like me? How can this be what you want for me? How can I be all that you created me to be if all of this heartache and suffering is going on in my life?"

Chapter 15

"The weapons we fight with are not the weapons of the world. On the contrary, they have divine power to demolish strongholds" (2 Corinthians 10:4).

I knew that the anger I felt toward my mother wasn't good and that I needed to forgive her, but I just couldn't. Not only had so much of my past hurts come from her, this new hurt was still so raw. During the next five years my son went to college for free where I worked which was an enormous blessing. I had serious bouts of depression and anxiety, but was trying to work through them. I had some amazing friends from my church who were there for me and knew a lot of what I was going through, which helped me to stay in prayer and keep seeking God through all of this. I got to the point where I thought I had forgiven my mother as best I could, but I still couldn't hear her name without getting a sick feeling in the middle of my stomach. I decided to go for therapy and deliverance counseling.

In my sessions with this wonderful woman of God, we worked through many of my issues including my past abortions, relationships, and my mother. She told me that God had forgiven me and I needed to do the same. *Forgive me?* I still had a long way to go in understanding how much God loved me and the life He wanted to give me, but it was a start. During one of our sessions, we were praying about forgiving my mom when all-of-a-sudden this feeling of a heavy weight just lifted off of me. I realized that the type of forgiveness I needed was only able to come from God and, at that moment, I knew He had touched me. Things started to change and they changed fast.

As I have so often noticed in my walk with the Lord over the years, when I press in and seek Him I begin to see wonderful things happen and other not so wonderful things creep up in an effort to discourage me. This is where spiritual warfare comes into play and I had a ways to go in learning about this. I was excited to see God move in my life the way He did. I was determined to press in and see him restore so much of what had been taken from my life. As I did this, our financial situation looked grim. They kept putting off the workers compensation decisions. They kept finding reasons to not come to a decision. It felt like they were putting it off in hopes we would give up. We were now going on seven years of waiting for a decision. We didn't have enough money coming in to cover all of our expenses. As hard as this was, looking back, every time I had a real need for my son or myself, it was always somehow met. I believe that God was providing and watching over us as David's stubbornness to accept God in his life took us down this rough and crazy time in our lives. I never would have been able to hold together through all of this without my faith.

One afternoon, I came home and David informed me that we were being evicted from the condo. We were a couple of months behind and he wanted us out. We put our stuff in storage. My son had to put his dog in the kennel and we went to my daughter's. David wouldn't stay there. He wasn't free to come home in the condition he usually came home in with his grandchildren there. He went and rented a cheap hotel room with the little bit of money that we had. Everything that I had tried so hard to hold onto and hold together seemed to be falling completely apart. I had absolutely no idea how anything could work out.

Two weeks after the session with my therapist when had I experienced that breakthrough, I was at work and on the verge of tears when my mother called me. She asked me how things were going and I broke down. I told her where I was living and what was going on and that I didn't know what to do. To my amazement, she told me that she was sorry for what she had done to us and that she felt she had to help me. She said if we could find a place she would help us with the money we needed to put down. I was taken aback by the timing of the phone call and the offer. I realized then that a stronghold had been broken when I truly forgave my mother.

We found a house that was bank owned. The bank just wanted to get rid of it. We were able to purchase it, with my mother's help, at a very reasonable price. I just knew by the timing, price, and location that God had provided this for us. The house had been on the market for over a year without an offer. They wanted to get rid of it, so the price had been reduced by $100K. The woman who owned the home had died and it was an estate sale. The house and everything in it was being sold "as is." We didn't care. We were just happy to have a place to finally call ours. Things moved fast and we were in the house within three weeks. The day we signed the papers, Jacob went and got his dog out of the kennel and we moved in. We had Thanksgiving dinner on paper plates with boxes all around us and a kitchen that was in desperate need of remodeling, but we were happy.

I was experiencing a new level of faith in my walk with the Lord. I still had such a long way to go, but I was starting to see that he was peeling off the layers of pain and hurt that had kept me bound for so long. I started to have this hunger inside of me to know the Lord more and more and to see Him use my life to glorify him. I couldn't shake this feeling and desire that He had so much more for me to experience and do for Him.

I started reading and studying the Bible more. I listened to tapes and programs of people that I felt were truly anointed of God and scripture based. I was attending a new church. David was still drinking and his health was deteriorating significantly. He was starting to swell with water and was having difficulty breathing. He was easily winded by just walking up the front stairs to our house. The doctors told David that if he didn't stop drinking, he was going to die. Even this didn't make him stop. I came home from work one day to find David in bed crying. He had been drinking so heavily and he just kept asking me to help him. I called places that would take him and help him to quit drinking. I made all the arrangements. Everything was ready. All I had to do was get him on a plane and they would meet him at the airport. Everything else was paid for by my insurance, but when he woke up the next day he wouldn't go.

My daughter Tia was now married with two boys. The highlight of my life was to have the boys over and spend time with them. David was becoming more and more abusive and easily agitated. One night when the boys were sleeping over, David became angry at something I had said to him and he proceeded to throw a glass full of vodka across the room, shattering it and sending the glass flying. The next day upon hearing this, my son-in-law said they couldn't come over when David was there. This crushed me. My family was, and is, the most important thing to me aside from my relationship with my Lord. Every time I made any headway in my life and things began to look-up, something would happen to try and steal that joy. I knew that God didn't want this pain in my life, but I didn't know how to change it. I wasn't sure if I should just leave. *What if he did try to kill himself again?* Even my friends and family didn't understand why I stayed. Something in me just broke and I had had enough. I was hurt, I was angry, and I was done.

Chapter 16

"He brought them out of darkness and the deepest gloom and broke away their chains" **(Psalm 107:14).**

We started attending a new church, a church that my son's youth pastor had a vision to start. It was an amazing church; a place that is so easy to feel like we belong. It has such a wonderful group of believers whose sole purpose is to reach others who are in need of knowing Jesus; living like Jesus lived and loving like Jesus loves. One Sunday, our Pastor presented us with a challenge. He had read a book called the *Circle Maker*. The book talked about a man called Honi, who drew a circle around himself and didn't leave until he got an answer to his prayer. The purpose of this challenge was to draw an imaginary circle around an area or areas of our lives that need to change or that we are having trouble with. He challenged us to fast and pray for a week over these needs. I had seen God provide and protect me my whole life. I knew that He didn't want me stuck in this situation the way I was, so I decided to go all out and take the challenge.

Every day at lunch, I took my Bible to the beach down from the university where I worked, parked my car, prayed, fasted and read. I told Tia and Jacob what I was doing and asked them to join me in this, to fast whatever way they felt led to and pray with me. That Friday at the end of my week of fasting and praying, David informed me that he didn't feel well. He was so swollen with water and was having such trouble breathing that he couldn't lie down and sleep. He had to sleep sitting up. I had hardly been speaking to David at this time. It was difficult not to get into an argument, so I decided not speaking was easier. David told our daughter that he was going to go to the hospital over the weekend and get help and they discussed the fact that they would probably have to put him through a detoxing program before they could help him. He said he was okay with that. That Saturday, the following morning, David drove himself to the hospital.

We went to visit David over the weekend and he seemed well. He was sitting up in bed, eating and talking and laughing with us. He didn't show any signs of distress at that point. Part of the protocol for aiding in alcohol withdrawal called for administrating a sedative, so they were giving David Ativan. The following Monday morning I went to work and I planned on going to see David when I got off. He called me during the day asking for lemons. He said he needed lemons for his water. I was confused and concerned by the phone call. He didn't sound like himself to me. He sounded almost as if he had been drinking for hours and yet I knew he wasn't. I went to see him that night and immediately I sensed something wasn't right. He was extremely agitated.

I had seen David go through withdrawals before, but it was never like this. Granted, he had been drinking more and for a longer period of time now, but I was still concerned. Talking to the nurses, they said that it was common for withdrawal patients to act like this. I assumed they knew what they were doing and assured David that he was fine before going home that night. Later that night, David called me, very upset, yelling that they didn't know what they were doing. It unnerved me, but I still believed that it was the withdrawal doing it to him.

The following day I took off and went to be with David. As much as I was upset with him for all that he had put me through, I still didn't want to see him go through this alone. The whole time that I was with David that Tuesday, he slipped in and out of consciousness. When he was conscious, he was extremely agitated, trying to rip the IV out of his arm, and take his clothes off. He wasn't making any sense and his breathing was becoming labored.

Finally later that afternoon, when my daughter was there, they sent an ears nose and throat specialist to check out his breathing. By this time though, she couldn't evaluate him because of his agitated state. Every time they attempted to wake him up to examine him, he thrashed his arms around, yelling, trying to leave the bed. I didn't realize at the time that the Ativan they were giving David was having an adverse effect on him. It was mimicking alcohol withdrawal symptoms and the more he reacted, the more Ativan they gave him. They were, in a sense, killing him and I was helplessly watching it happen.

I felt as if I was numb all over. I knew what was going on wasn't good, but I had no idea how to help. Everything was spinning out of control and I remember thinking, *Lord you're in control but I really don't understand why this is happening.* David was finally going to get some much needed help and it seemed to be backfiring. I knew that David had caused so much hurt to his children, to myself, to other people, and even to himself. I also knew how much hurt he had suffered in his life. If

God decided to take him home no one would have been surprised. If he lived however, how would God ever be able to repair and restore what was so broken?

Chapter 17

"...and provide for those who grieve in Zion—to bestow on them a crown of beauty instead of ashes, the oil of joy instead of mourning and a garment of praise instead of a spirit of despair. They will be called oaks of righteousness, a planting of the Lord for the display of his splendor" (Isaiah 61:3).

David was finally beginning to put together the pieces of what had happened to him and he was starting to remember things from his own perspective. One day as we were talking about what had happened, he started to remember the night that his heart stopped for those twelve minutes. He didn't remember anything that happened up to that point. He did however remember the doctors around him saying, "We are going to have to call this." He says that he knew his body was dead, but he was totally aware of what was going on around him. He remembers saying, "No, I'm not ready" and thinking about his children and me and that he needed to get back to us. He told me that he felt two presences, one that wanted him to die and one that wanted him to stay. After those twelve minutes, all goes blank in his memory and he only remembers bits and pieces as he was coming out of the coma emergence state over the next few months.

A very dear friend of ours came over to visit David and gave him his own Bible. David started going to church again, only this time it is different. He starts reading his Bible. He volunteers at outreaches at our church. He attends Bible study classes and seems to be absorbing all that he is learning with a hunger that is new to him. David is very much glad to be alive. He has a different outlook on everything.

Over the next year and a half, David made amazing progress. It seemed like every day there was something else he wanted to do on his own. As he became more independent, he informed me that he wanted to be able to drive himself around and not sit home every day while I am at work. This caused me a lot of anxiety. First of all, I was not even sure he was well enough to drive.

We also learned that one of his corneas was damaged and he needed a cornea transplant. During the twelve minutes that David's heart stopped, his body functions began to break down. Blood flow began to cease and neurological pathways in his brain started to deteriorate. The doctors were concerned about his reaction times and his reflexes. *Were they quick enough for him to respond to actual driving situations that could come up?* I took him to several doctors to be evaluated. Every doctor that evaluated David was totally amazed at the progress he had made and that he was doing so well. That he even came out of the coma was a miracle in itself they said. Even so, I was not convinced that he was physically able to drive. I was also concerned about where he would go and what he would do. *Would he go back to where he used to hang out and start drinking again?*

By this time, I had seen so much of what God had done that I decided to let David go and leave him in God's capable hands. I learned that my worrying and trying to control everything just didn't work. A friend of mine from church came up to me one day and told me that the Lord told her to tell me something. I was amazed at what she said. She told me not to be afraid to let David go; that God was totally aware of all that concerned me and to trust that he was holding David. David had the cornea transplant and it was a complete success. He went for a driving test, something that is required when there is a brain injury involved, and he passed.

David use to enjoy going to a tavern down the road, drinking and talking to the owner, and watching the news. They had become close and would discuss world issues and all the stuff that was going on. Being brought up in the bars as he was, this was a familiar and comfortable scene for him. As he becomes more comfortable with driving, he informs me that he wants to go see Harry and watch the news with him. My first reaction is to be fearful. *Would the temptation be too much for him? Would he fall back into his old habit?* As I was praying about it, I had this strong sense that God was telling me once again to let him go. He couldn't work anymore, he wasn't drinking, and he needed to be able to do the things that he enjoyed. He enjoyed talking to Harry and seeing people he knew. A peace that I can't describe came over me and I never really worried about it again. Once in a while when the thought did cross my mind, I dismissed it, and placed him back in my Father's hands.

Over the next six months, David started working on our house. He put in a stone walkway and redid the landscaping in the front of the house. He also put in a large paver patio in the backyard. He took over the bills and finances and for the first time in our married life he made sure everything was paid on time.

Saying you forgive someone can sometimes be easy, but truly forgiving from the heart requires a lot. From my own experience, I can say with conviction that it takes something supernatural. David was changing in ways that were amazing, but he was also still David. Each time he did or said something hurtful, I slipped back into my old thinking. *I've been through enough with you. Why do I still have to put up with this?*

There were many things in David's life that were old habits that needed to be changed. I could so easily see them. What wasn't so easy for me to see were the things in my own life that God wanted to change. I didn't accept criticism easily. I was always a shy, introverted person. I was consumed by my own feelings of insecurity. I never realized that this was a form of pride and something that could hinder me from being everything God wanted me to be. I struggled from early on to put my life together in my own strength. I was strong-willed. Regardless of why or how I became that way, I knew I needed to change. As I began to work on myself, I started to see a change in David. He was always the type to speak what he thought, mostly without thinking about it, which would easily hurt or offend others. Saying he was wrong or sorry has never been an easy thing for David. He would rather let it go and hope that it would be forgotten. He started to tell me that he was sorry for what he had done and that he hadn't been there for the children and me all those years. He admitted he hadn't provided for us the way he should have and that he should have been more thoughtful about the future. Hearing him say these things I asked God to help me let go of every root of bitterness and to love David the way God wanted me to.

Chapter 18

"Give thanks to the Lord for he is good; his love endures forever" (1 Chronicles 16:34).

They say hindsight is 20/20. As I sit and think about my life and especially the last few years, I am blown away by not only the perfect timing of everything, but by the unconditional love of our God. How very much he cares about all of us, down to the smallest detail of our lives. Many times it has been the small things that made me realize just how much our God loves us. Looking back through all the difficult times, the times when there wasn't any money coming in, or when they repossessed my cars, or turned off my utilities, or even when I lost the homes I was living in, I can honestly say I have always had everything I needed. Someone always showed up with food, or clothes, or money. I was never left on the street. They were very difficult times and I'm sure because of the many wrong choices that I made things happened the way they did. I'm reminded of the Israelites in the wilderness for forty years. They were there for disobedience, yet God led them by a pillar of clouds during the day to protect them from the heat and fire by night to warm the cold desert evenings. Their shoes never wore out and their feet didn't swell.

God's provision went far beyond our material needs. I am well aware of the pain of a child growing up in an abusive environment, whether emotional or physical. I have covered my children continuously in prayer since they were born. The reason my children turned out as amazingly wonderful as they did is because of His promises to us - to be a father to the fatherless and a husband to the husbandless. Although my children's father was there, he wasn't around much for them. They could very easily have gone the wrong way and rebelled and messed up their lives, but they didn't. I know I owe that all to Jesus, who heard every prayer I prayed.

In raising my children in the faith and taking them to church, I formed friendships with other couples, usually the parents of my children's friends. There were times when I would be envious of the women who had godly husbands that took their faith seriously and were there for their families. One morning in prayer, I was talking to the Lord and I told him how I felt about that. As clear as day a thought came to my mind, "I have been that for you. If you had that with someone else, you would not be where you are with me today."

God brought David back from the dead. He has regained so much of his physical abilities. His brain and thought patterns have been restored. After the cornea transplant, David received back his vision as good as new. Most of his strength has been restored and he has become such a blessing and important part of our family.

Of all the things that I have seen God do, bringing David back from the dead is not the most amazing to me, as incredible as that was. To me, it has been the transformation of the man. God did in an instant what I had tried so hard for thirty some years to do. David is now trying to be the best father, husband, and grandfather he can be. He goes to church because he wants to. He's studying the Bible and attending classes. He prays with me for our family and others. I'm not embarrassed or ashamed by what he is doing. He is sober and enjoying his life and for the first time is truly alive. I finally have peace in my home.

It's not that God wasn't with me throughout my whole life. In fact, it was just the opposite. And it wasn't that He wanted me to go through so much pain and heartache to teach me something. It was me who was having trouble receiving God's love and mercy. In my early childhood I was taught to be fearful of God and that the horrible things that happen in this life are His will. I grew up with criticism, abandonment, and a lack of intimacy that made it very difficult to understand God's love for me. It wasn't because my parents were horrible parents. They weren't. They could only give me what they knew and what they had been taught. My life experiences caused me to see God as a critical, harsh, and cold being who was watching to see if I would mess up, waiting to inflict some kind of punishment on me. Nothing could be further from the truth. His word says you shall know the truth and the truth shall set you free. Fear causes bondage not freedom. Through his patience and amazing grace he began to peel back those layers of pain and start to heal my wounds. His desire was for me to be everything he created me to be, but first he had to get me out of the way.

I am excited because I know it is just the beginning. Yes, even at my age, it can be just the beginning. It really is never too late. The layers of hurt and oppression are being removed. When someone mentions to me about all the time and the heartache I went through and why did it have to take so long, I tell them I believe that God is so good and desires to bless us. I also believe that if He just blessed us without teaching us, much of what He does would be lost, because of how we are. Do I think things would have been easier if I had listened to God when he told me not to do something? Definitely! Or when such a heavy feeling would come on me and I would know what I was doing was wrong and yet I still did it? Absolutely. The fact that He never gave up on me and kept drawing me back to Himself is just His amazing abundance of grace!

As I watch the transformation that is taking place in me, the grip that I have on my own life is loosening. I am giving Him control because I know He loves me. As I continue to pray and seek God and study His word, I am amazed at the depth of His love for us and the riches of His glorious inheritance that he so eagerly provides for us. As I learn to trust, He pours His healing balm over the broken jagged pieces of my soul and I begin to get a glimpse of who I am in Him. I am the righteousness of God in Christ. I am in Christ. As He awakens my spirit to new revelations of who He is and who we are in Him, I am consumed with such a hunger and thirst for more of Him.

I heard somewhere that the greatest form of worship there is, is to trust God with all you are and all you have. That is the place where we enter into His rest. I am now just beginning to understand how to enter that rest and receive the good things he has provided for me. In turn, he has not only given me the desires of my heart, but he is giving me the desires of His heart for others and the desire to help reach them so they also can be free.

An Abundance of Grace

Listen to Lynn Kavanagh's

Interview on

<u>Chronicles of the End Times.</u>

Recommendation.

The <u>Hidden Thrones</u> series by Russ Scalzo is a suspenseful, inspirational, and biblically accurate account of end time events that are prophesied to happen in the near furture…a must read!

Sincerely, Lynn.

Made in the USA
Middletown, DE
23 July 2018